THE ART OF
TERMINATOR SALVATION

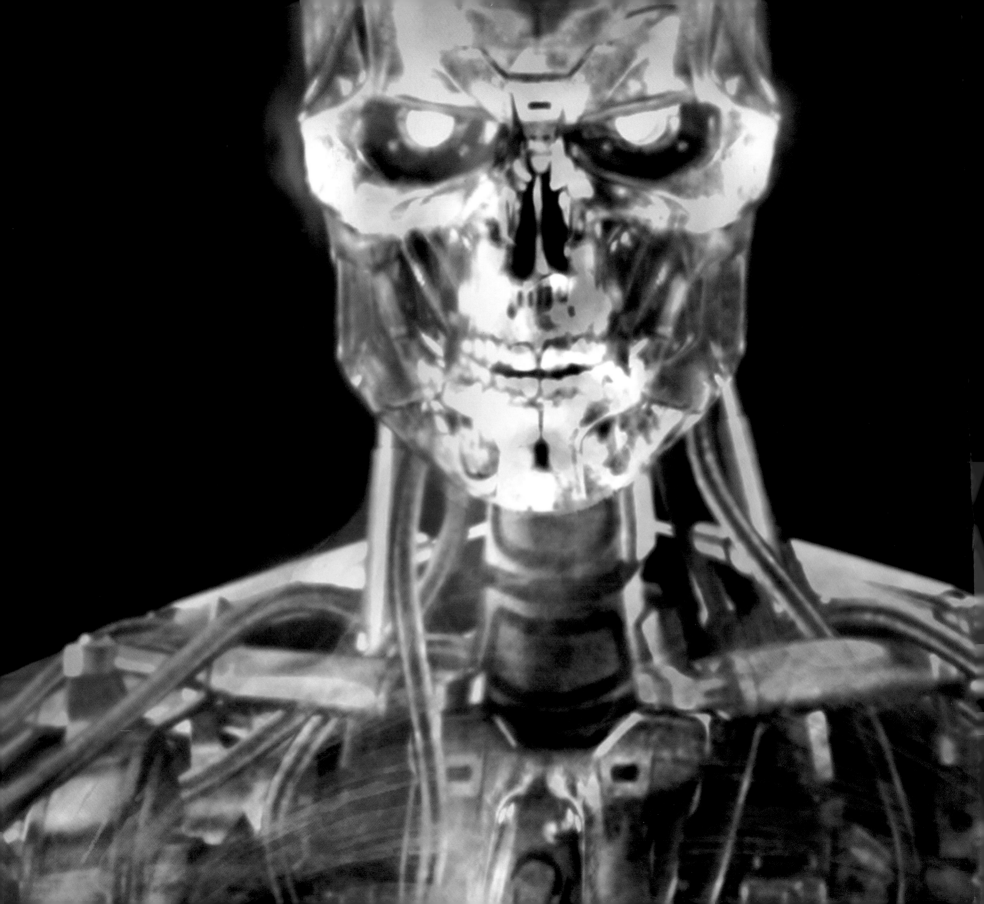

THE ART OF

TERMINATOR SALVATION

BY TARA BENNETT

TITAN BOOKS

THE ART OF TERMINATOR SALVATION

ISBN: 9781848560826

Published by

Titan Books

A division of

Titan Publishing Group Ltd

144 Southwark St

London

SE1 0UP

First edition April 2009

2 4 6 8 10 9 7 5 3 1

Terminator Salvation ™ & © 2009 T Asset, LLC.

Visit our website:

www.titanbooks.com

Titan Books would like to thank McG and Martin Laing for their enthusiastic co-operation with this book. Thanks also go to the many supremely talented people who worked on the movie or the video game and helped with this project: Renier Banninga, Martin Bergquist, Andy Chung, Tim Flattery, Steve Gordon, Peter Johansson, Marty Kline, Cos Lazouras, Dave Lowery, Victor James Martinez, Robert McKinnon, Adolfo Martinez Perez, Erik Pettersson, John Rosengrant and Stan Winston Studio, Ted Slampyak, Jason Sweers, Dan Sweetman, Miles Teves, Michael Wilkinson, and Victor J. Zolfo.

Did you enjoy this book? We love to hear from our readers. Please e-mail us at: readerfeedback@titanemail.com or write to Reader Feedback at the above address.

A CIP catalogue record for this title is available from the British Library.

Printed and bound in China by C&C Offset Printing Co., Ltd.

This spread: Production designer Martin Laing's concept art of Skynet's stronghold in San Francisco.
Next spread: Early concept art by Adolfo Martinez Perez.

INTRODUCTION

The world is an arid wasteland. The rusted-out carcasses of long-dead vehicles litter the landscape, too many to count. The air is thick, choked with smoke as random fires burn in the distance. A tooth-rattling rumble is the harbinger of never-ending streams of terrifying machines that crash, crush and shoot their way through the empty streets of once vital cities. And then there are the lone machines, silver horrors with blood red mechanical eyes that stalk the last vestiges of humanity after Judgment Day.

Ask any cinephile to name the film in which that post-apocalyptic world resides, and there's no doubt you'll hear *The Terminator*. Twenty-five years ago writer/director James Cameron introduced audiences to his nightmarish, cautionary tale of a future where machines have taken over the world and hunted man to the brink of extinction.

In the years since, it has spawned two blockbuster sequels — *T2: Judgment Day* and *Terminator 3: Rise of the Machines* — made Arnold Schwarzenegger an international star, and remained a seminal mythology on the potential nightmare of a post-nuclear tomorrow. Yet none of the films has actually taken place in that post-apocalyptic world. Each has provided fleeting, harrowing glimpses and nothing more...until now.

Terminator Salvation dives headfirst into the future that had only been described to Sarah Connor in the harsh, whispered stories of Resistance soldier Kyle Reese. Gone are the contemporary settings of the previous films. The future is *now*, and John Connor is a grown man who exists to stay alive in a world teeming with Terminators.

With the creative canvas laid bare in front of them, director McG, production designer Martin Laing, director of photography (DP) Shane Hurlbut and Stan Winston Studio set out to do nothing less than breathe reality and life into a future untapped. From their collective imaginations unfurled desolate post-nuclear landscapes, horrific new Terminator models, and even the birthplace of hell on Earth: Skynet.

As directors James Cameron and Jonathan Mostow did with the previous *Terminator* films, McG mined the deep mythology of the franchise to find inspiration in shaping a bold vision for his film. Yet before launching into pre-production, McG says, "I first started by checking

Previous spread left: A T-600 stands guard.

Previous spread right: Inside the Stan Winston Studio workshop.

Right: Production designer Martin Laing and friend.

Opposite: Early concept art for the T-600.

in with Jim Cameron and talking to him about what I intended to do. He granted me his support and said how he felt a similar way when making the second *Alien* picture, following Ridley Scott. He wanted to honor Ridley but at the same time give the film his own imprint. I wanted to do that too, so I took every step possible to facilitate separation from the other pictures and create our own film. It began with creating our own film stock, our own film processing and a post-apocalyptic world that's designed to feel absolutely real.

"I also thought it was critical to begin again, to honor the mythology of the first three pictures, but certainly to begin again," McG continues. "What made the story worth telling in my eyes was the simple fact that this is the first post-Judgment Day *Terminator* picture. All the other films were present day with Terminators coming back in time. This film happens several years after the bombs go off, in 2018. We get a look at Skynet and a look at the machines that were the beginning of the T-800s, which is the Arnold Schwarzenegger model. We also see Harvesters and Hunter-Killers and Aerostats and Hydrobots — all in the pursuit of destroying humanity."

The mandate above all others on *Terminator Salvation* was to strive for realism, be it the right amount of dirt on a uniform, or the oil coating the moving parts of a T-600 on patrol.

The person McG hired to achieve that goal was production designer Martin Laing. A frequent collaborator of James Cameron, Laing says, "The great thing about being a fan of the first three movies, and having spent a lot of time with James, was that I was very invested in the project before it even started. It has a foundation and history, and the marvelous thing is that we are building on that history. Here we have the great luxury of actually going to Skynet and revealing that post-apocalyptic landscape we've only really seen in glimpses before. Here we are able to live in the world of what has happened after Judgment Day and explore what is behind the whole franchise — what is behind the Terminators. In the world that we are in,

we are before the future seen in the first three movies, so we can look at different machines being made. In the previous films, there have been the T-800 Terminator, the silver T-1000 and then the female Terminator T-X. But pretty much it's always just been one or two characters. Here we have created another eight or nine different Terminators to add into the mix. We are touching a lot of the points that all fans will know and love, but we are building on that and creating a new world. It's not Terminator 4; it's *Terminator Salvation*."

While the previous *Terminator* films lived in contemporary times and were crafted to work as both sci-fi and action-thrillers, McG made it immediately clear to his creative team that *Terminator Salvation* would be a gritty, desolate war film. John Connor and the Resistance survive in a broken-down world of scraps and decay, and audiences need to feel that desperation. "It's designed to be as tactile

Laing's concept art of a devastated Los Angeles was his first painting created during pre-production. It sparked the team's first real production design ideas for how to portray this post-apocalyptic world.

and real as possible," McG explains. "We did all the research we could possibly do at Chernobyl, and with futurists about what the environment would look like after a nuclear bombing, what the sky temperature would read like and what would happen with the lack of an ozone layer. It was everything that would go into the look, feel, taste, touch and smell of this world."

Early in 2008, the creative team got together to start hammering out this aspect of the film. Laing says those first days were flush with an inspiring mix of creative output.

"We were in a situation where there was a writer's strike, and we couldn't get the script rewritten, so we all sat around and came up with fun ideas," Laing remembers. "The first thing I did was the devastated Los Angeles painting. I did that very, very quickly, but it really brought on

the conversation of what this world was going to be. And the great thing about this film is that it has been such a team effort. For my part, I came up with the idea of making the Terminators dark. I said, 'We don't have to make them silver — the whole "silver sci-fi silliness" as I call it; we don't have to go down that road. Let's bring it more into reality.' I think you want to try and ground things when you are making a sci-fi movie and make it as real as possible, so people can actually relate to the world you are creating. So now our Terminators are made of steel. As if you went to an old locomotive train yard, and you saw the beautiful, strong, steel structures of the trains and how things were cast. They are very oily, very metal and very, very dark, and that's the world of our Terminators here. It's a grittier and darker movie, but yet it has that sense of reality as well."

Director of photography Shane Hurlbut developed the other key element in fleshing out the film's overall look with the use of a color-grading technique called "The Oz Process." Laing explains, "It's a digital format. It's the same process you use when you are developing black and white film, where you put the [image] through a silver bath quite a few times."

McG continues, "Basically, we're adding three times as much silver as you would normally add to a color stock. It's almost as though you would take a color stock and run it in the way that Ansel Adams would do a large format black and white print. It gives it a patina where you don't lose any detail of the blacks — it just has this 'other' quality that makes it feel like we're looking at a world that isn't contemporary."

Paired with the raw, otherworldly locations found in the remote deserts of Albuquerque, New Mexico, *Terminator Salvation* now had a signature look that added a new dimension to the storytelling. "[The Oz Process] is great for the landscapes, because you don't see the bright blue sky and the big yellow sand. Everything gets desaturated and a layer of silver is added on, which gives a bizarre look," Laing says. "When we first started we were planning to shoot in Budapest. We flew to Hungary, spent some time there, and then flew to Croatia. But when you read a *Terminator* script you don't automatically say, 'Let's go to Budapest!'" he laughs. "We then brought it back to America and the barren landscape of Albuquerque was fantastic, and much easier for us. You just have these rolling expanses that go on forever in this arid desert."

Production art showcasing the striking desert locations to be found in New Mexico.

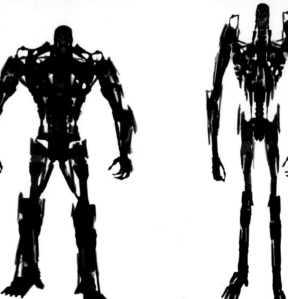
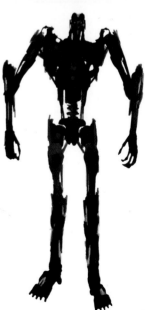

TERMINATOR SALVATION
TERMINATOR CONCEPTS
VICTOR MARTINEZ 01.24.08

VICTOR MARTINEZ
2008

With the aesthetic in place, Laing says McG then handed him the creative reins to maintain a strong guiding hand in the concept art and design. "One of the things I set forth when I started was that this is a movie 'designed by Martin Laing.' And that means it had to be designed in the art department. I'm not ever-so-keen on branching things out to different design houses because it never gels. It never looks the same."

Laing continues, "So when we designed our T-600s — our really tall Terminators — we were able to blow them up full size and deliver art to Stan Winston Studio and say, 'This is it. This is the blueprint you have to work with.' The same thing with the Hydrobot — we designed it and blew it up full size and handed it off to them. They then went through the process of making it into a 3D form. And Stan Winston and his crew have been absolutely wonderful. They brought the dream into reality." Pausing solemnly, he adds, "It was so sad that we lost Stan early in pre-production, but the crew has done an amazing job. They knew the history of *Terminator* and were able to use a lot of their technology to bring our 2D drawings to life."

By production's end, Laing and his team had created almost one hundred concept paintings and countless technical drawings. Those McG-approved designs then went to their creative collaborators like Stan Winston Studio, ILM (Industrial Light & Magic) and Asylum Visual Effects, where the cohesion of design remained consistent until the final picture lock.

Appraising the overall artistic journey of *Terminator Salvation*, Laing asserts that the creative team challenged one another to make a film that would stand apart by being a bold new voice in the *Terminator* mythology. "McG did push and expect a lot," Laing admits. "But then I am *very* self-critical, and I will push and push to make sure that what appears on the screen is what I want it to be in terms of the look. If I do a painting I want the set to look like that painting. I don't want to sell McG on a look that I can't deliver. When you create a look, you want to get it up onto the screen, and happily we have been able to do that quite a lot here."

In this book, the creative team further explains the evolution of the visual world of *Terminator Salvation* through concept art, storyboards, technical drawings and production photos. Their words provide an insider's perspective on the process of taking a vision of the future previously left only to the better part of audiences' imaginations and making it real. Welcome to *The Art of Terminator Salvation*.

Opposite top: Production art for the scene in which Marcus escapes from the Resistance Outpost.

Opposite bottom: Early concepts for the new Terminator models introduced in the film.

Left: Laing's team delivered full-size blueprints of the T-600 to Stan Winston Studio.

EXECUTION

The film opens with death row murderer Marcus Wright (Sam Worthington) being prepared for his execution. "He's given up on himself," McG says of the character. "He's given up on humanity. The world that we all know has treated him cruelly. He's in jail and he's ultimately put to death." Yet before his execution, Marcus signs over his body to scientist Dr. Serena Kogan (Helena Bonham Carter).

The sequence was shot at Santa Fe prison and Martin Laing explains that the now derelict facility helped shape the entire opening. "We wanted to covey that bird in a cage look. We wandered through [the prison] and took some inspiration of what it must be like to be incarcerated in this bizarre place. And this is the one part of the movie when you get to see normal color. Everything after this is post-Judgment Day, with the 'Oz Process,' so we wanted to keep the colors richer and that's why we went for the warmer tones."

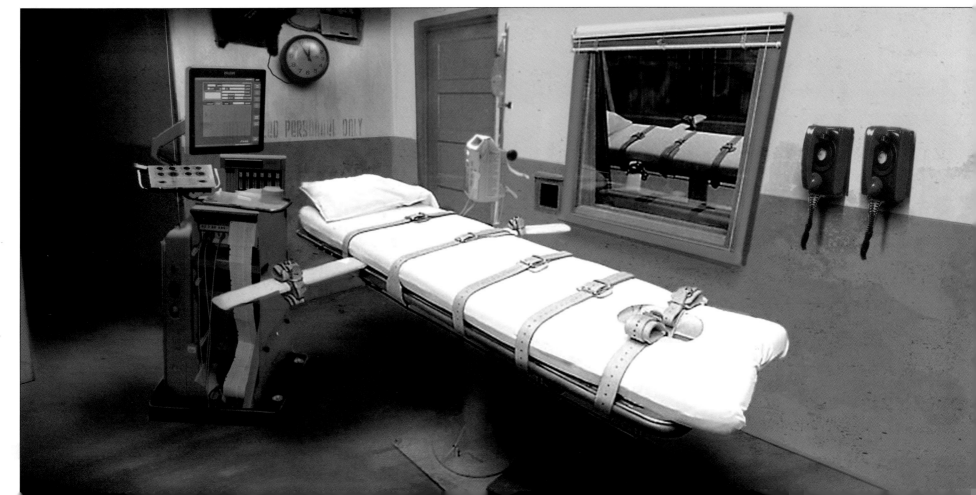

From Marcus' execution the film shifts to 2018 where an intense firefight at the VLA (Very Large Array) is in progress. These storyboards by artist Dave Lowery illustrate the dramatic moment of a flaming soldier felled in the melee. Almost immediately the skin melts away to expose the terrifying endoskeleton beneath. It's a Terminator – a T-600.

Moments later a helicopter skid lands on the skull, crushing it. A boot then appears in frame and the muzzle of a gun explodes into the skull of the writhing Terminator. The camera tilts up and the hero is revealed – John Connor (Christian Bale).

It's an intentional twist on the iconic Terminator image of an endoskeleton smashing a human skull seen in previous films. And McG says it immediately sets the tone in terms of introducing the kind of man this post-apocalyptic John Connor is. "To me, an actor's entrance is critical," McG explains. "You always want to introduce each actor with a memorable entrance. From the back of the neck with the mysterious scar on it in *Pulp Fiction* to John Connor's helicopter landing on a T-600, I am a big fan of classic cinema language. But we go on and the fun from here is that we realize that John's not the leader. He's a foot soldier who has respect and loyal men and women that serve under him, but he's by no means the leader of the Resistance. We'll see how through fate and his own clever sense of deduction he becomes the leader of the Resistance. And we learn all that in the first minute of him being onscreen."

When designing the look of the Resistance vehicles, Laing explains that he wanted everything to look piecemeal and haphazard. "Their world is a very textured world – a patchwork quilt. The vehicles they use, the airplanes they use and the helicopters they have are all an amalgamation of bits and pieces. For instance, if we have five Hueys and only three of them work, the other two are stripped for their parts. The door might have a red color on one and green on another."

Costume designer Michael Wilkinson says that he absolutely wanted to reference the costuming choices used in previous films to help tie *Salvation* into the *Terminator* franchise. Specifically with John Connor, Wilkinson went for a subtle connection. "Eddie Furlong, the young John Connor in *Terminator 2: Judgment Day*, wears tiger stripes," Wilkinson explains. "In our movie, we thought it'd be fun to have tiger stripes also on Christian Bale. You can see the tiger stripe pants that he wears when we first see him in the film. It's a nice little nod to the previous incarnations of John Connor."

Yet aside from that choice, Wilkinson says that he deferred to Christian Bale's ideas for this grown-up John Connor. "When I met with Christian it was evident that he was very much into understatement in his costuming. He didn't want to overplay or telegraph with the costuming, which I think is a fantastic approach. He wanted to have his costumes as simple as possible and as streamlined as possible, so he only has two or three looks for the whole film. We are also living in a world where people have very limited resources. So I'm very happy with the result because he has a stealthy, almost ninja quality. As the film became more and more about him rising to the top of the Resistance, he wanted to show that he was just one of many other soldiers and there was nothing outstanding about his appearance. I think it was a really good impulse."

UNDERGROUND
FACILITY

Previous spread: Artist Dave Lowery's storyboards of John Connor entering the vast pit of Skynet's underground facility.

As John and his men enter a storage room, the eerie light of a flare illuminates hundreds of ghastly human Skynet prisoners in pens. "The bars, the incarceration, the overcrowding – there's nothing nice about this place," Laing says of the designed environment. "People are stuffed into cells and we are saying that humans in this world are the cattle. It's a world of people looking wide-eyed off into the darkness. You only get a glimpse of their faces as you go by and it's scary. These sets are mainly in the dark and only illuminated by the flashlight on the bottom of the rifle, so that makes it scarier."

Laing designed very stark, sterile worktables equipped with robotic arms for Skynet's gruesome experimentation on its human prisoners. Whether they are grafting steel to horribly amputated limbs or harvesting skin for R&D, the tables are in effect butcher blocks for humans.

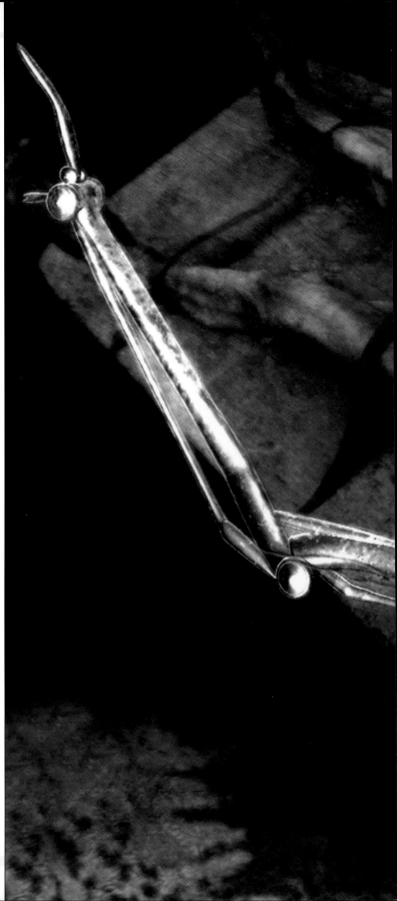

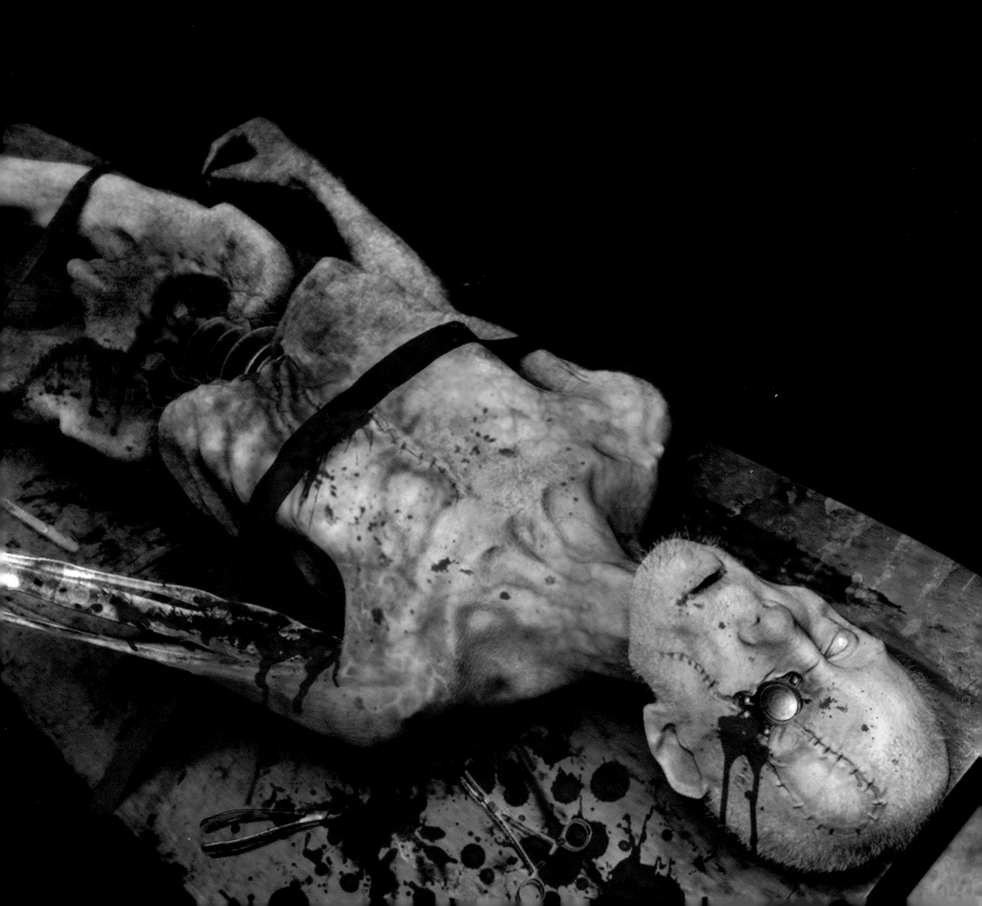

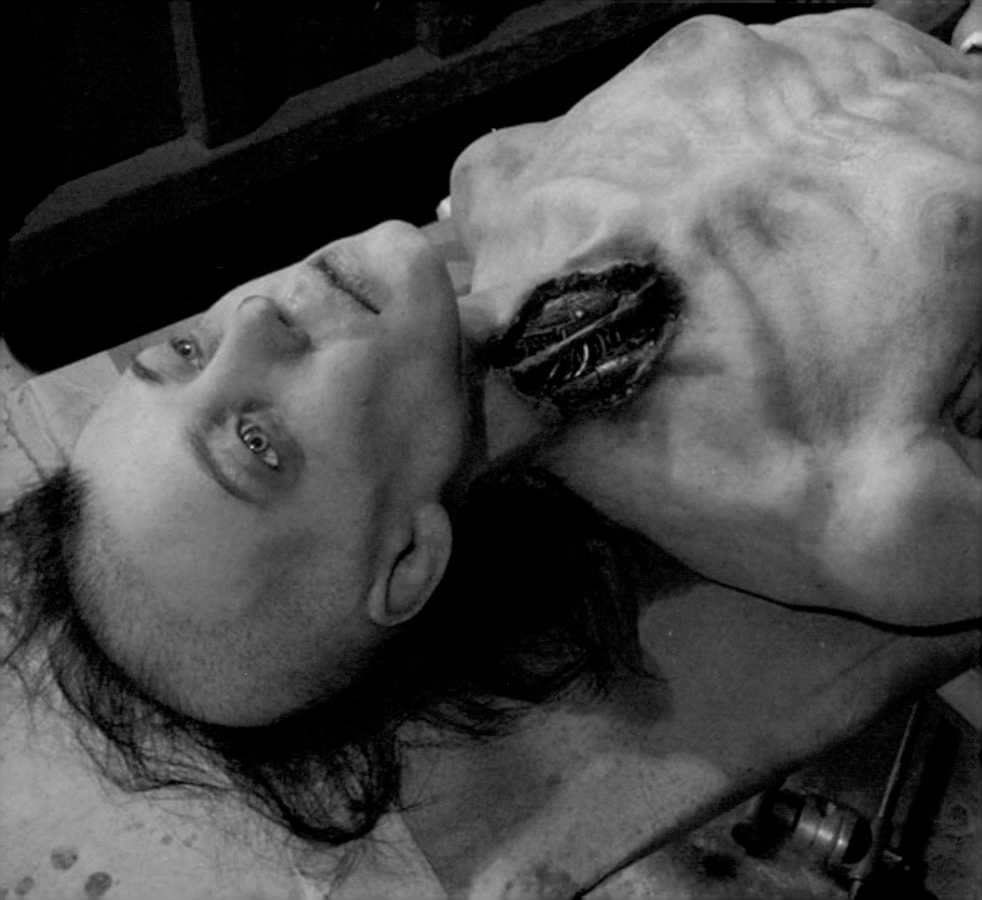

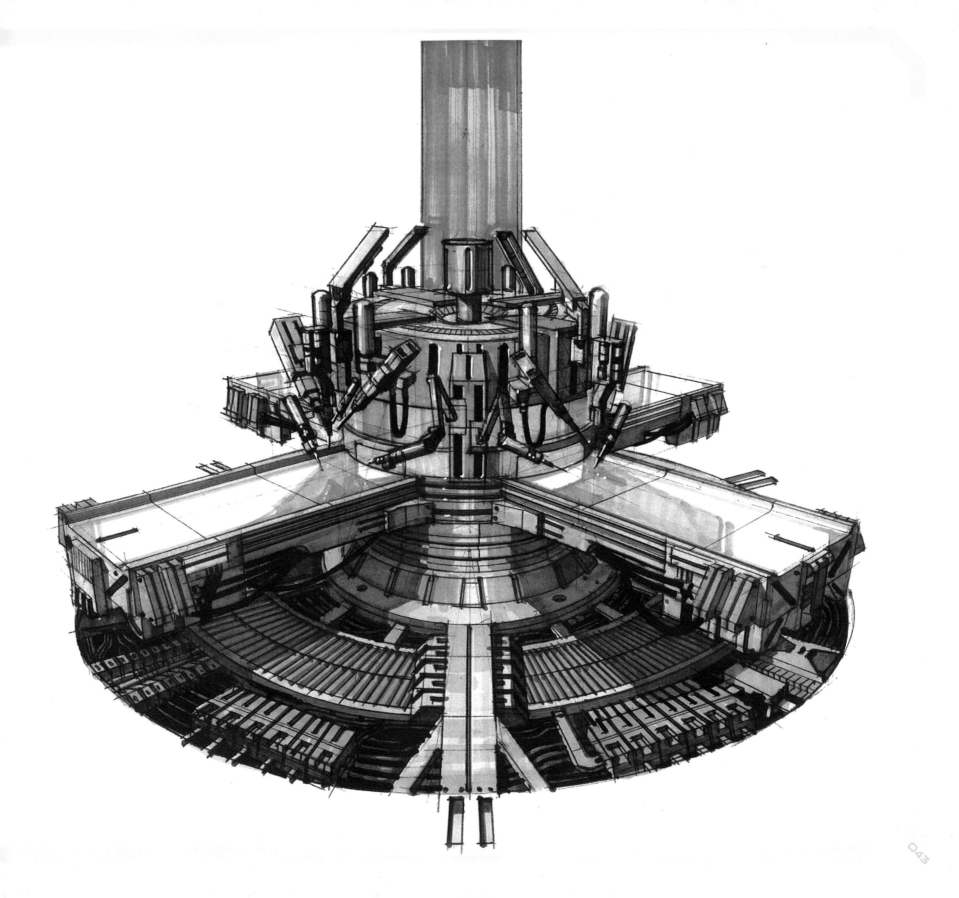

The T-1 model first appeared in *Terminator 3: Rise of the Machines* and reflected the futuristic silver aesthetic of the Terminator designs in that film.

For *Salvation*, the T-1 model was dirtied up to reflect the dark future of a world run by machines. Laing explains, "Our world is a lot more brutal so we took the same kind of idea, that it is literally a machine gun that will come after you, and brought it into our world."

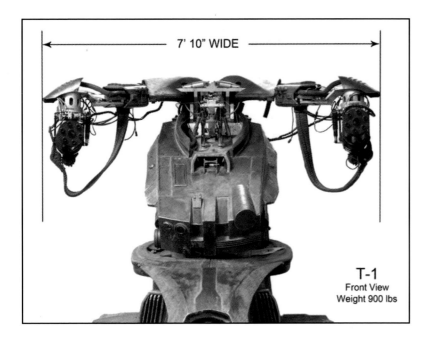

7' 10" WIDE

T-1
Front View
Weight 900 lbs

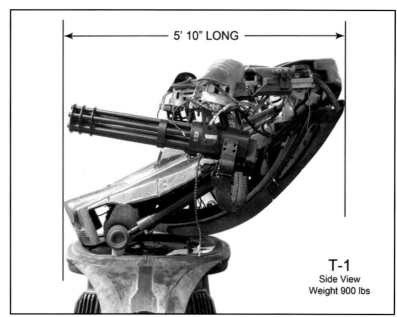

5' 10" LONG

T-1
Side View
Weight 900 lbs

As John and his men scour the underground facility, a T-1 rises from the water. Laing explains the T-1 design: "We were inspired by the structure of a Chieftain tank, and added the armaments used in real-life war weapons of today. We gave it the versatility of these wonderful 500-round Gatling guns on top that would mow you down. It's a machine that's purely there to kill you. It doesn't have to look pretty — just ominous."

Martin Laing's concept art of John Connor escaping the massive implosion of the Skynet Communications Complex.

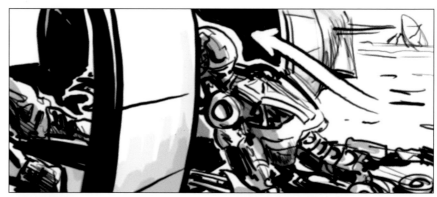

This storyboard sequence shows an injured John frantically crawling towards his helicopter as the badly damaged torso of the T-600 relentlessly drags itself forward to stop him. It's a dire situation that plays out very similarly to the one Sarah Connor survived at the end of *Terminator*. McG explains, "We always looked for ways to elegantly respect the films that came before this. This seemed appropriate and we thought, 'Hey, look at the way the mother and son battles echo one another.' I think it's something you hear a lot in real life when a parent says they remember when they were their kid's age and they went through something similar. It's a fun way to explore similar struggles over space and time."

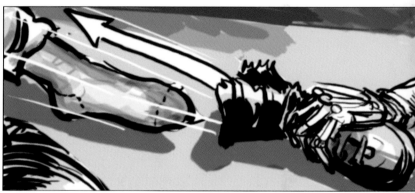

In this solemn concept art, Laing explains the theme was "adding insult to injury." "Here the mission has been completely compromised," he explains of John's forlorn stance. "He's lost all of his men and been in the battle of his life with a severed T-600 that's relentless. On top of all of that when he's finally finished, it starts pouring with rain. It's a very sad environment that doesn't get any better. Then he disappears off into the dark."

The violent storm that envelopes John also portends the unexpected return of Marcus Wright. In the original painting (opposite), Laing explains, "We're very high on Marcus looking down, very much like that famous shot of Tim Robbins in *The Shawshank Redemption*. On the day of the shoot we had this whole array of helicopters and blown up pieces from the battle so we were able to compose this wonderful shot that wasn't as high." McG and director of photography Shane Hurlbut then added the rain, which Laing says "worked more as a birthing scene…it's that rain that washes the mud off of him — it's the cleansing birth of Marcus."

SEA COMMAND

After John is picked up by the Resistance in a helicopter, the location shifts to the storm-lashed ocean. The storyboards and concept art show John dramatically jumping into the roiling waters. Laing explains, "He is picked up by a submarine. That's a clever move by the Resistance Command. That's how they have been escaping from Skynet — underwater."

MARTIN LAING '08

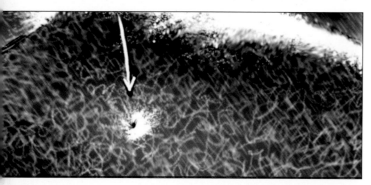

INT. OFFICERS' WARDROOM / SUBMARINE
"CONFERENCE AREA"

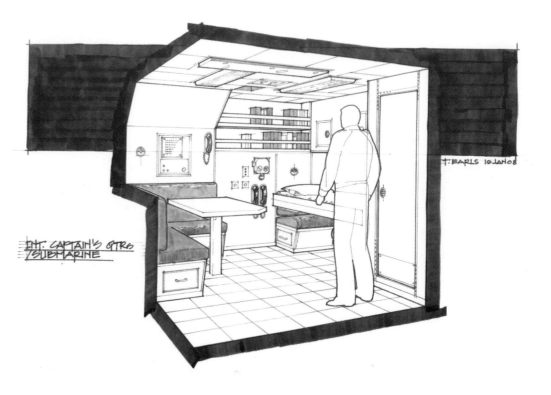

INT. CAPTAIN'S QTRS / SUBMARINE

The production actually filmed inside a Los Angeles class submarine, which the design team then dressed to reflect the lack of resources at the disposal of the Resistance engineers. "We are in a world that is ten years old since the bombs went off," Laing details. "The sub hasn't been able to resurface and be repaired. It's a nightmare of cables all over the place because they have to survive with what they have. They are the pirates of the sea."

Uncertain of his purpose or location, Marcus, having taken clothes from a fallen Resistance soldier, travels miles and miles until he arrives in post-apocalyptic Los Angeles. The bleak tableau reveals the scale and scope of the nuclear devastation on what used to be a thriving city. Laing says nature played a big part in his overall design approach. "We are saying that ten years after Judgment Day a lot of the humans have left, so Mother Nature has now taken over. Mother Nature is obviously very strong, as we've seen with Chernobyl and in Japan after the bombs, and foliage is the first thing to come back. So although the devastation to the buildings is very apparent there is a softening of the edges from the foliage. We've also put in this underlying layer of red that shows the cancer – the bizarreness of the radiation. In Joshua Tree [National Park, California] many, many years ago there was a freak rainstorm and then two weeks later poppies grew in the desert, which no one had ever seen before. It's that same reaction that Mother Nature has to this world. There is a strange fauna, a red glow that blankets the area where the devastation and the radiation are the highest. Then as you come out of those areas and away from where the bombs went off, the red dies down again. It's a fun little tweak we did."

Terminator Salvation
Marcus LA Freeway
Andy Chung/ Martin Laing 08

LOS A
CITY
POP 3

069

Concept art of Marcus spotting a T-600 for the first time. Moments later Kyle Reese (Anton Yelchin) dives onto Marcus to save him from the predator. Kyle's first line is a familiar one: "Come with me if you want to live."

Laing explains, "The T-600s, which are our new soldier models, are designed to kill. They are purely monsters. The precursor model to the T-800, they are much less refined in terms of their human design. The T-600s were sent out into the field to start trolling for humans. They don't sleep or eat. They are machines that keep going with power packs that last for years, so it's the rain, the wind and the oil that give them their natural patina."

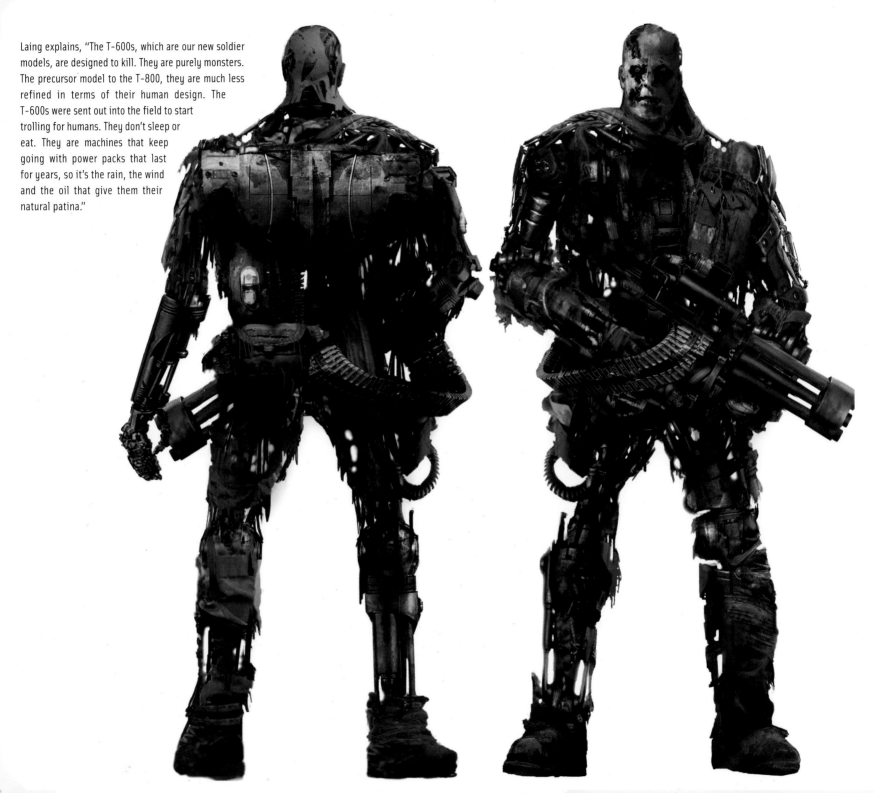

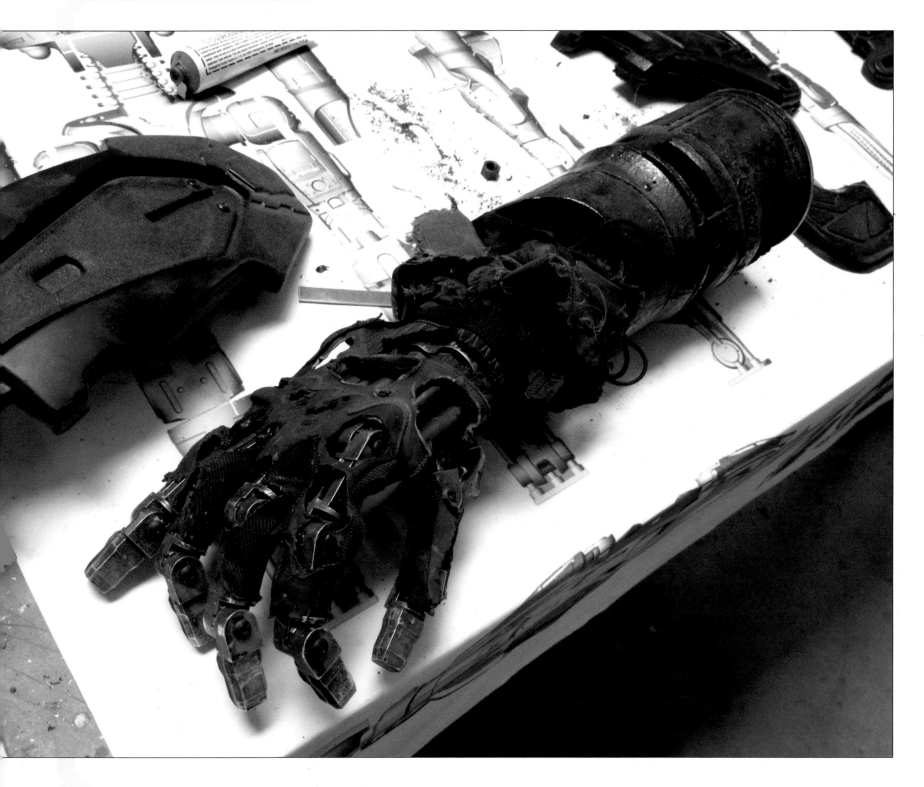

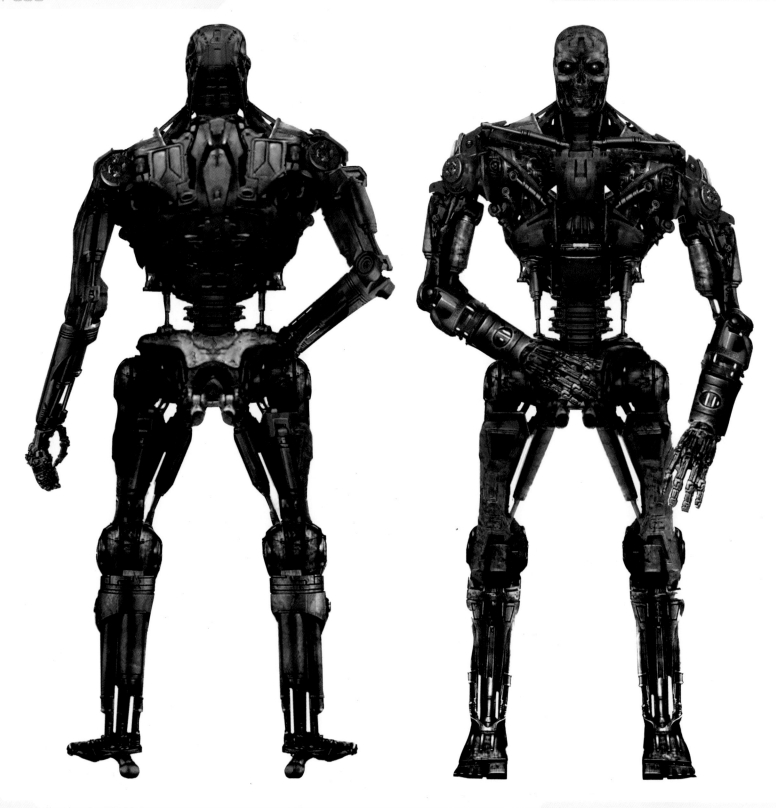

Laing adds that the T-600 design evolved from references made about it in the original film. "Kyle Reese [Michael Biehn] jumps in the car with Sarah Connor [Linda Hamilton] and says, 'The 600 series had rubber skin. We spotted them easy.' We took those elements and put them into the movie so it's part of the storyline. Our Terminators are bulkier...and they have the rubber masks, so there are a lot of boxes we are ticking off in regards to the whole mythology behind *Terminator*."

PATTON

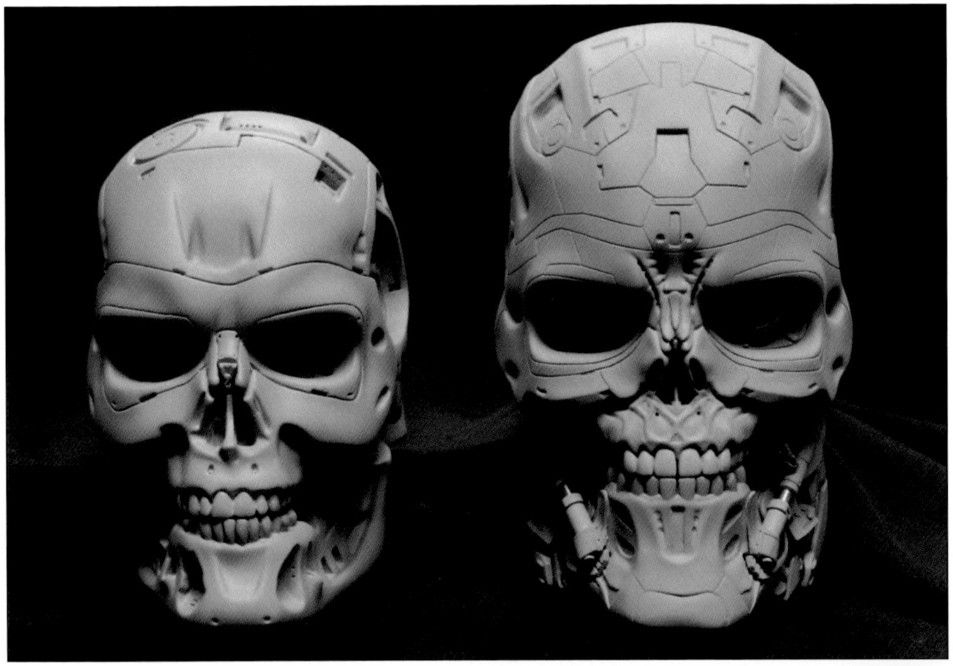

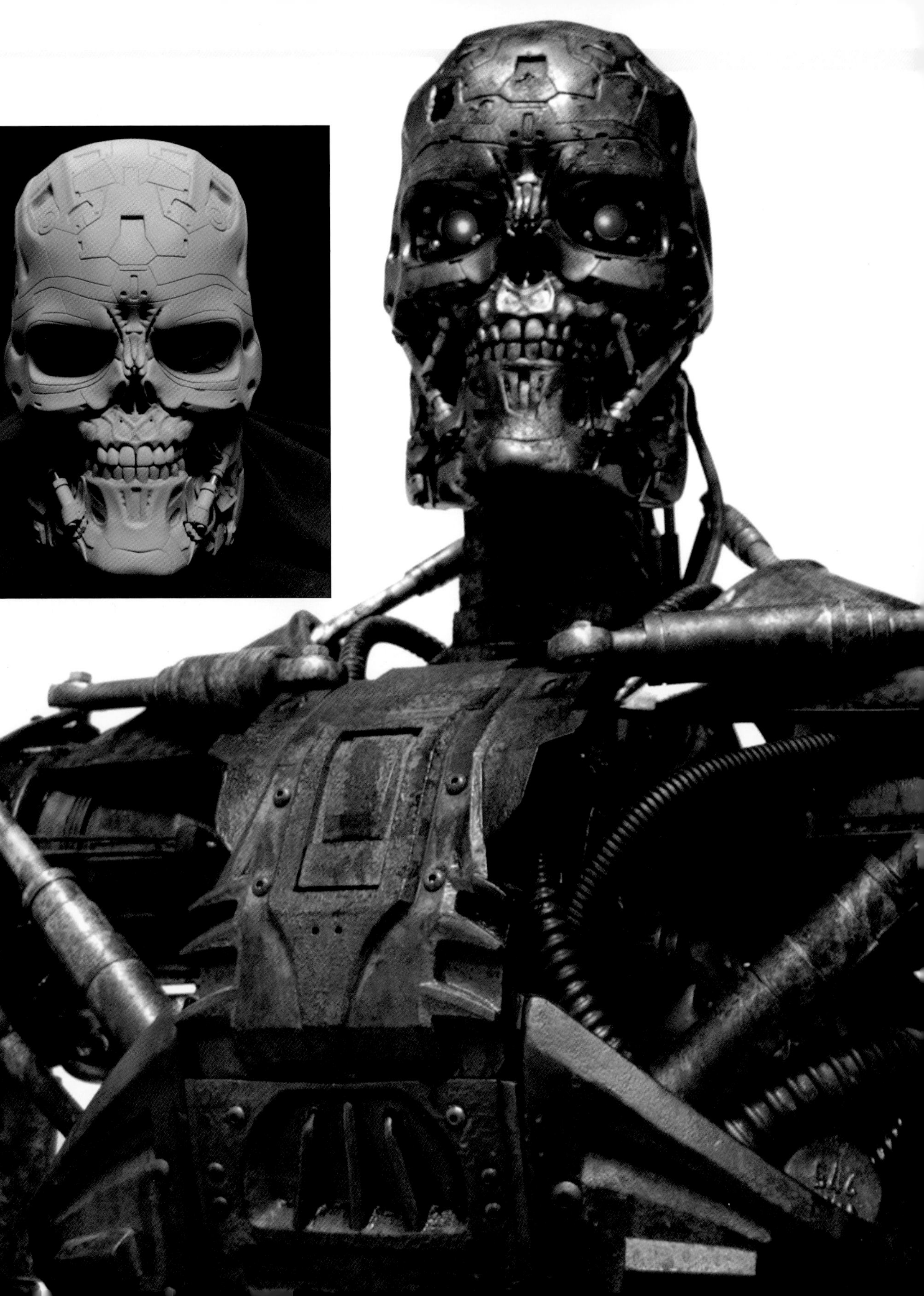

John Rosengrant, the animatronics supervisor at Stan Winston Studio, expands on the telltale physical distinctions of the T-600. "It's the bigger, more brutish version of a T-800 [see skull size comparison, opposite]. The idea is that the T-600s are all out in the field. They've been out there for years, nobody servicing them, so they're kind of battered and weathered. These are the first Ts to try to pass as human, but they are easy to spot, with a simplistic rubber skin that's been pulled over the face to camouflage it, and rag-tag clothing to hide the endoskeleton."

Michael Wilkinson says that young Kyle Reese's (Anton Yelchin) layered look is supposed to evoke the idea of "a homeless person that carries his whole life around with him. He doesn't know when he wakes up in the morning where he's going to be at the end of the day, so he's ready for anything."

As for Star (Jadagrace), Wilkinson says, "All of her clothes are adult clothes that are too big for her, so your heart goes out to her. She feels like she's a lost girl in this very adult world."

HUNTER-KILLERS

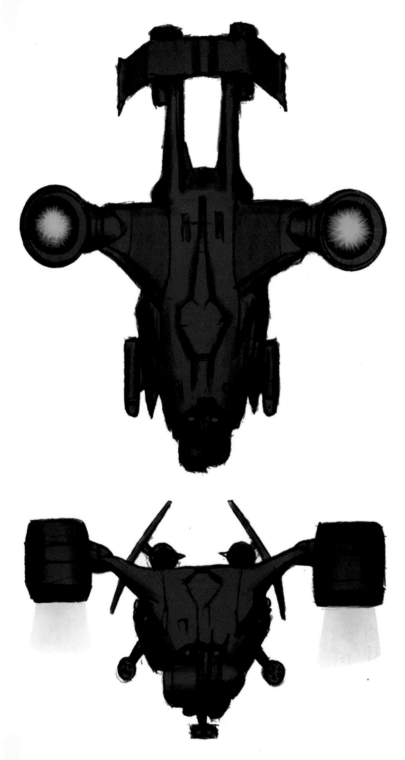

The Hunter-Killers, or H-Ks, are the aerial and ground patrol machines first described by Kyle Reese to Sarah Connor in *Terminator*. With their massive floodlights and infrared motion tracking, their singular function is to find humans on the ground and exterminate them. In *Salvation*, Marcus, Kyle and Star manage to go undetected by lying still while an H-K flies overhead.

While the final look of the H-Ks had a general template based on their appearance in the previous films, Laing and his team experimented with different designs for the aircraft (as seen in these images) since they played a bigger role in several key scenes in *Salvation*.

Interestingly enough, the one engineering issue that most affected the *Salvation* design of the H-K revolved around how the machine flew in the previous films. "Based on the H-Ks in the first three films, we knew that we had to work within the same Vertical Take Off and Landing (VTOL) way of flying," says Laing. "We had to design our H-K around knowing that it had to be reverse engineered in the same way as the T-600 was from the T-800. But we also went off on a tangent and tried to come up with our own different ideas. Eventually I took the illustration and reworked it into the final one. I wanted to make it more like a stingray, so it had more of a flowing line. I came to the final illustration retaking and reworking all the elements that we had and bringing into the final shape those which worked best."

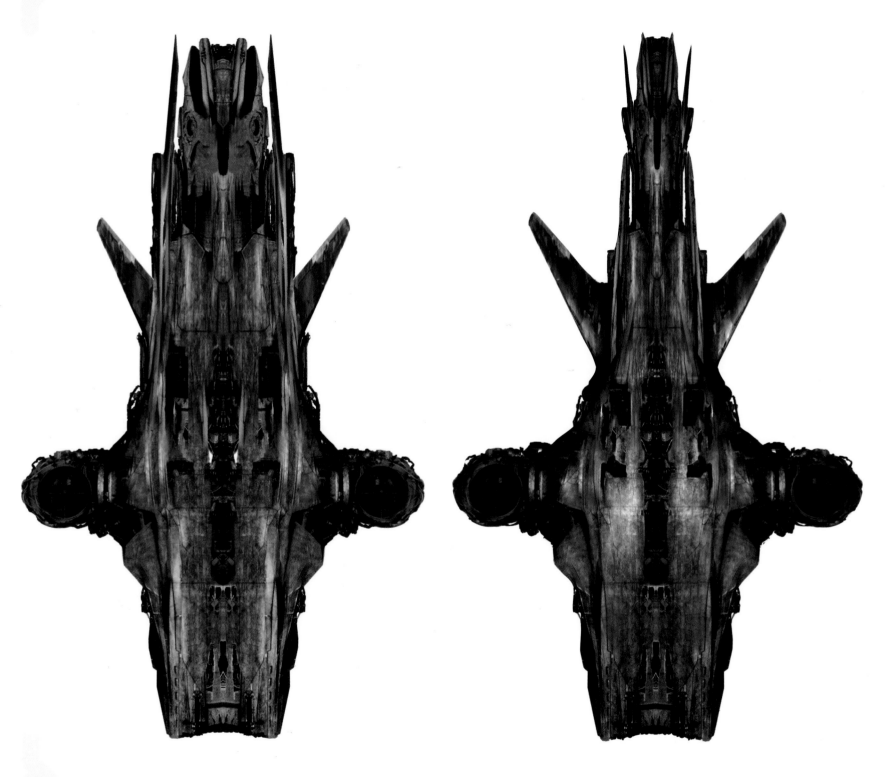

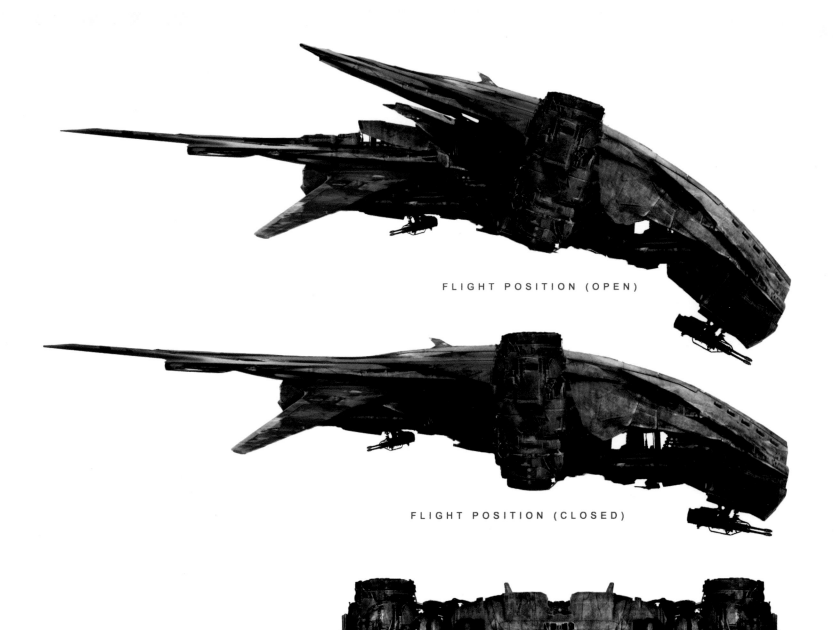

FLIGHT POSITION (OPEN)

FLIGHT POSITION (CLOSED)

The final look of the *Salvation* Hunter-Killer turned out to be a more streamlined version of the original. For McG's part, he enthuses that the final CG model of the concept art is one of the most dynamic machines in the movie. "The Hunter-Killers feel completely realistic. I can't believe in the final analysis that they weren't shot practically on the day – that's how real they look."

GRIFFITH
OBSERVATORY

Below are panoramic images of Laing's location scout of Griffith Park Observatory in Los Angeles. While searching for a place to create the makeshift home for Kyle and Star, Laing says, "McG, Shane and myself came up with ideas about what are the iconic buildings and areas within Los Angeles. One of the initial schemes was to use the Staples Center in downtown. But the feasibility and logistics of shooting it turned into a bit of a nightmare. At that point, Griffith Park came up. It's close to L.A. and they have a view of the city from the gardens. And the location also has a wonderful link to *Terminator*… it's where the T-800 robs some punks of their clothes."

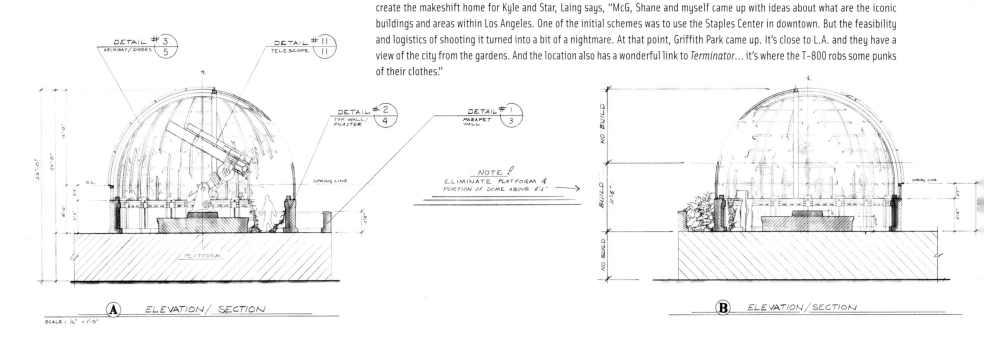

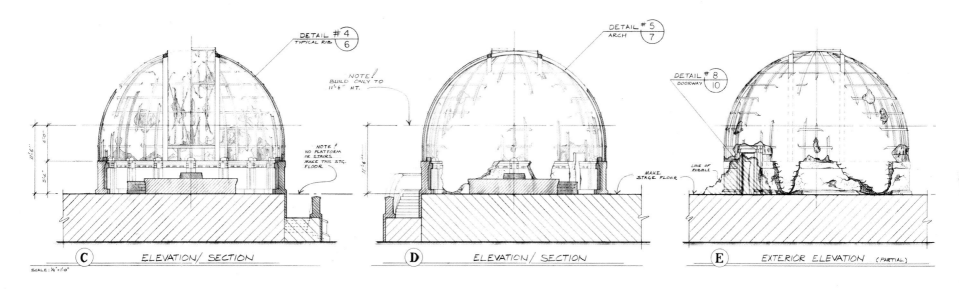

SCALE : ¼" = 1'-0"

DETAIL #4
TYPICAL RIB
6

Ⓑ ELEVATION / SECTION

DETAIL #5
ARCH
7

NOTE!
BUILD ONLY TO
11'-6" HT.

NOTE!
NO PLATFORM
OR STAIRS.
MAKE THIS STG.
FLOOR.

DETAIL #8
DOORWAY
10

LINE OF
RUBBLE

MAKE
STAGE FLOOR

Ⓒ ELEVATION / SECTION

SCALE : ¼" = 1'-0"

Ⓓ ELEVATION / SECTION

Ⓔ EXTERIOR ELEVATION (PARTIAL)

GRIFFITH

Inside the Observatory dome, Laing says that he wanted the pair to fill the space with their personalities.
"They are sleeping underneath the telescope and they are using a lot of things they have found in the streets
to decorate their 'house.' We have to remember these are kids: Kyle is fourteen and Star is five-ish. Therefore
she has these shiny bits that she finds, pebbles and broken sunglasses and such, to dress her space."

The concept images of the Jeep on the right reflect the patchwork vehicle that Marcus brings back to life
so the three of them can escape the city.

T:SALVATION   JASON SWEERS [08]

AEROSTAT

These are early concept paintings of the Aerostat reconnaissance robot. Its function is to search the landscape for humans and, when found, scan them with imaging lasers so the data can instantaneously be sent back to Skynet. The designs on this page reflect a more organic design direction with the robots looking more like insects than machines. "In the sketches and paintings, it has insect legs that can come down," Laing explains, "but we don't see that in the movie. We only see them flying."

Martin Laing explains that the Aerostat design came from an unexpected incarnation of the mythology. "If you look at *Terminator 2: 3D Battle Across Time*, which was the 3D movie James Cameron did for the Universal Studios theme park, he has these flying football sentries that go through the air searching for people. We used that for the beginning rounds [of design] and then worked out from that."

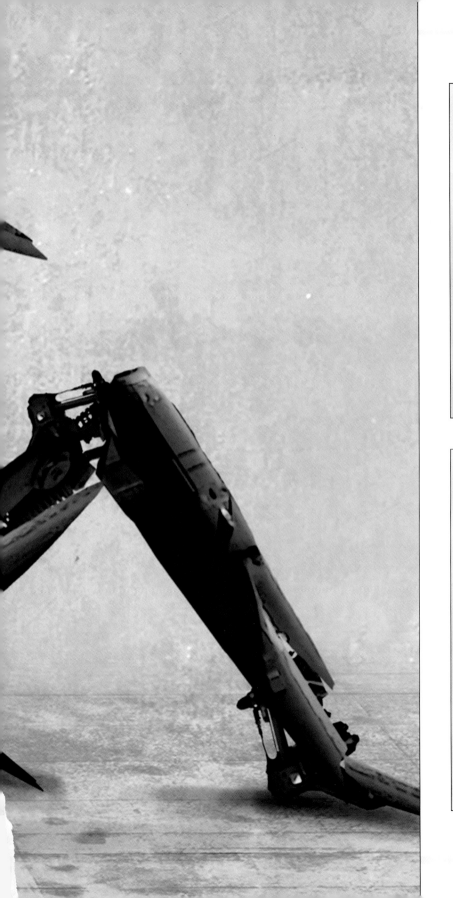

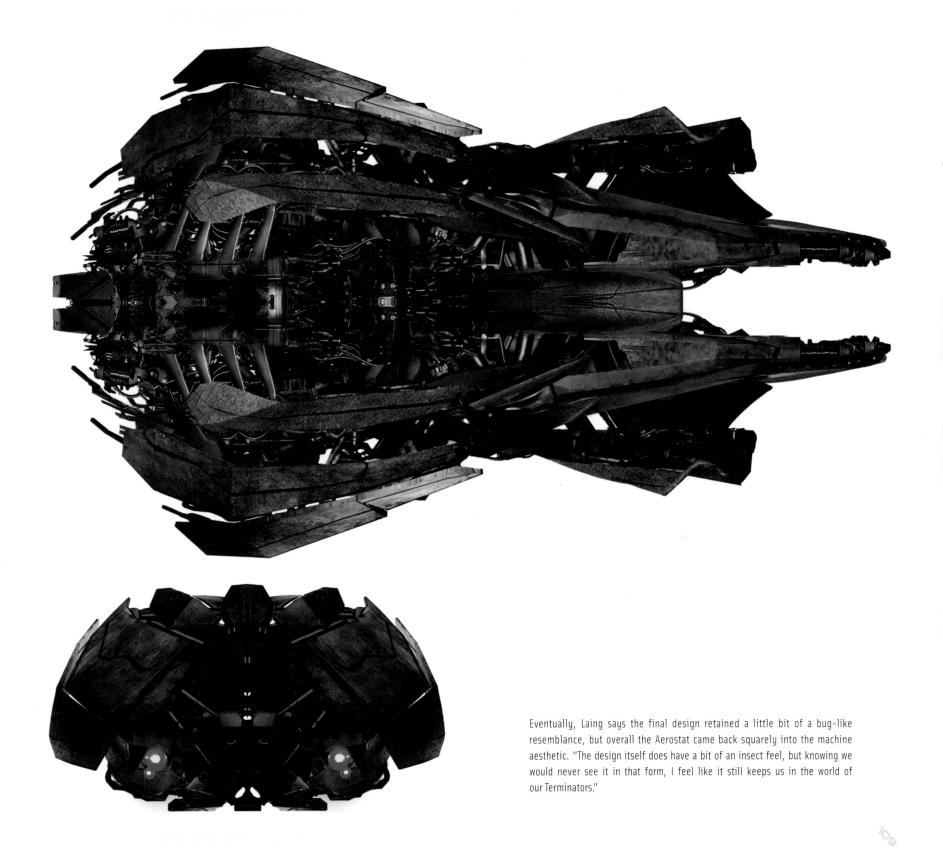

Eventually, Laing says the final design retained a little bit of a bug-like resemblance, but overall the Aerostat came back squarely into the machine aesthetic. "The design itself does have a bit of an insect feel, but knowing we would never see it in that form, I feel like it still keeps us in the world of our Terminators."

This storyboard sequence blocks out the intense chase of an Aerostat in pursuit of Marcus, Kyle and Star as they barrel down an embankment in the Jeep. The middle panels show the robot is able to get an image scan of the passengers in the vehicle before Marcus is able to hit and smash the robot with a precisely thrown wrench.

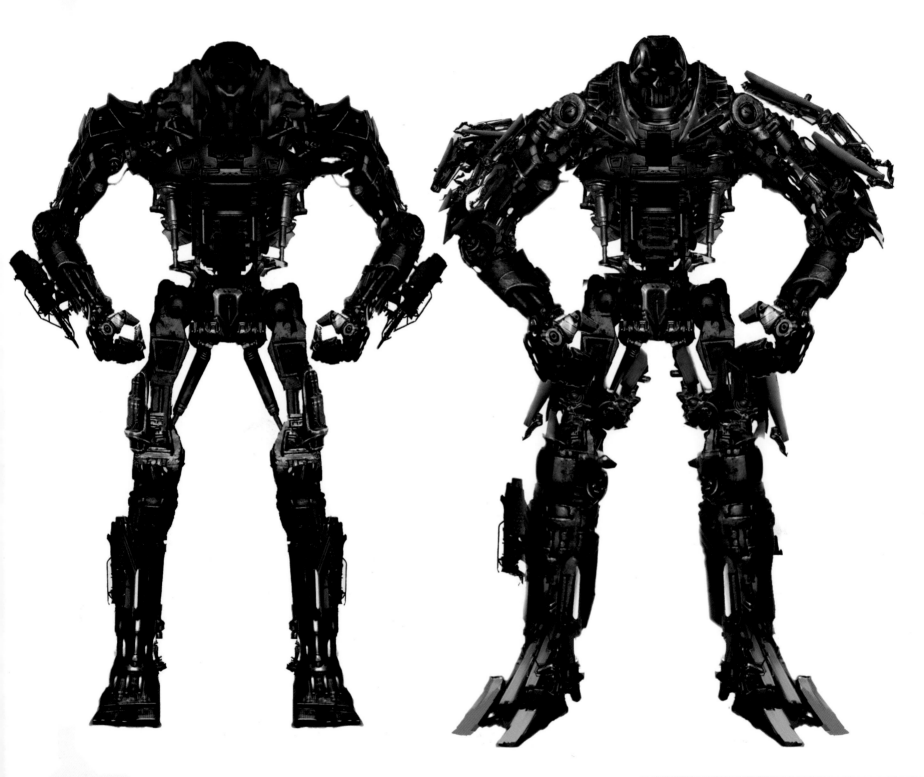

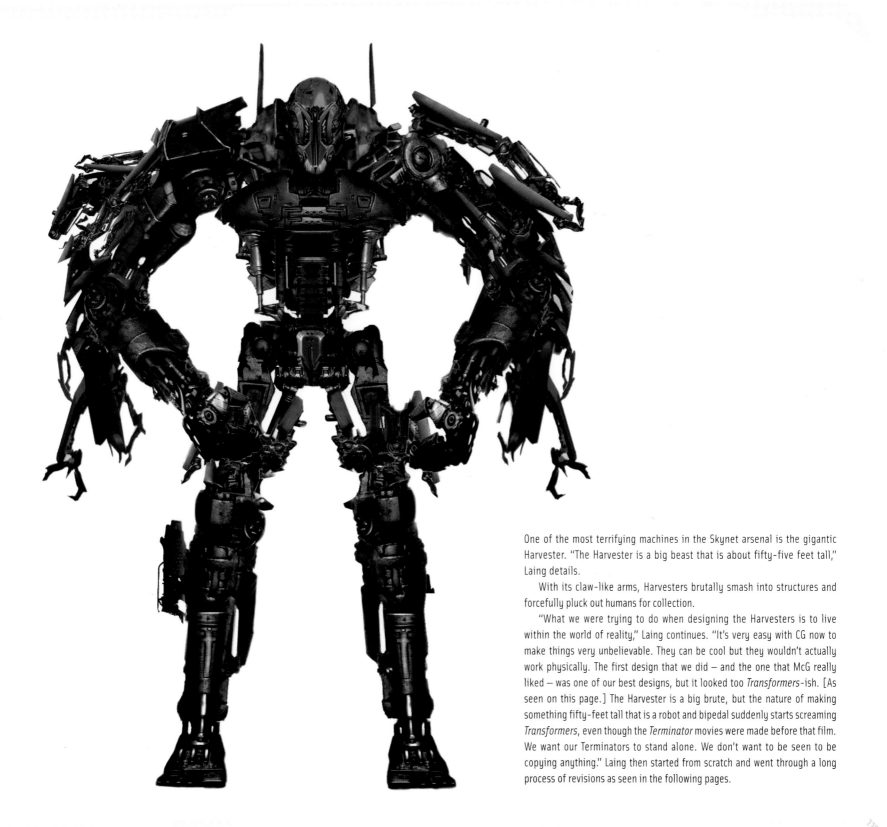

One of the most terrifying machines in the Skynet arsenal is the gigantic Harvester. "The Harvester is a big beast that is about fifty-five feet tall," Laing details.

With its claw-like arms, Harvesters brutally smash into structures and forcefully pluck out humans for collection.

"What we were trying to do when designing the Harvesters is to live within the world of reality," Laing continues. "It's very easy with CG now to make things very unbelievable. They can be cool but they wouldn't actually work physically. The first design that we did — and the one that McG really liked — was one of our best designs, but it looked too *Transformers*-ish. [As seen on this page.] The Harvester is a big brute, but the nature of making something fifty-feet tall that is a robot and bipedal suddenly starts screaming *Transformers*, even though the *Terminator* movies were made before that film. We want our Terminators to stand alone. We don't want to be seen to be copying anything." Laing then started from scratch and went through a long process of revisions as seen in the following pages.

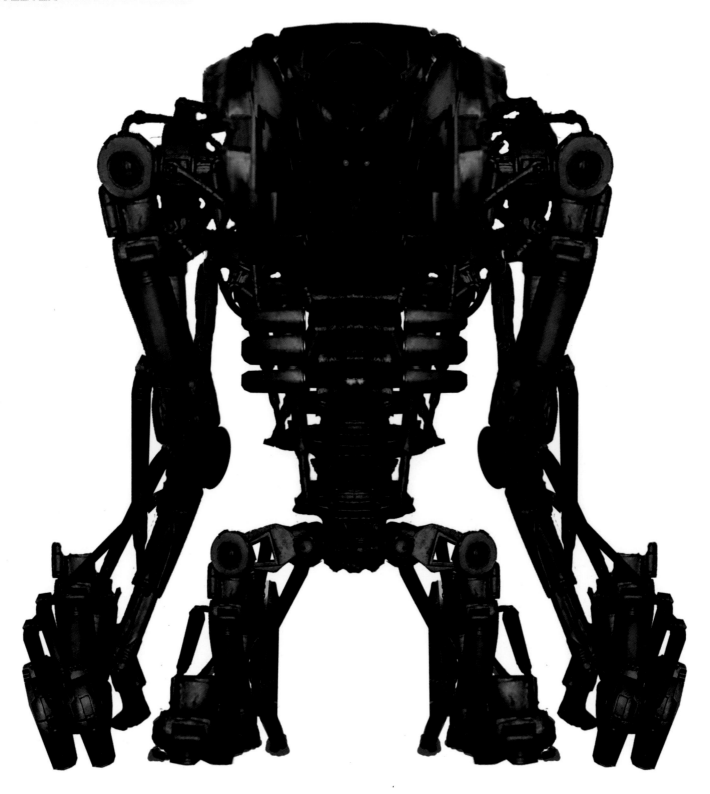

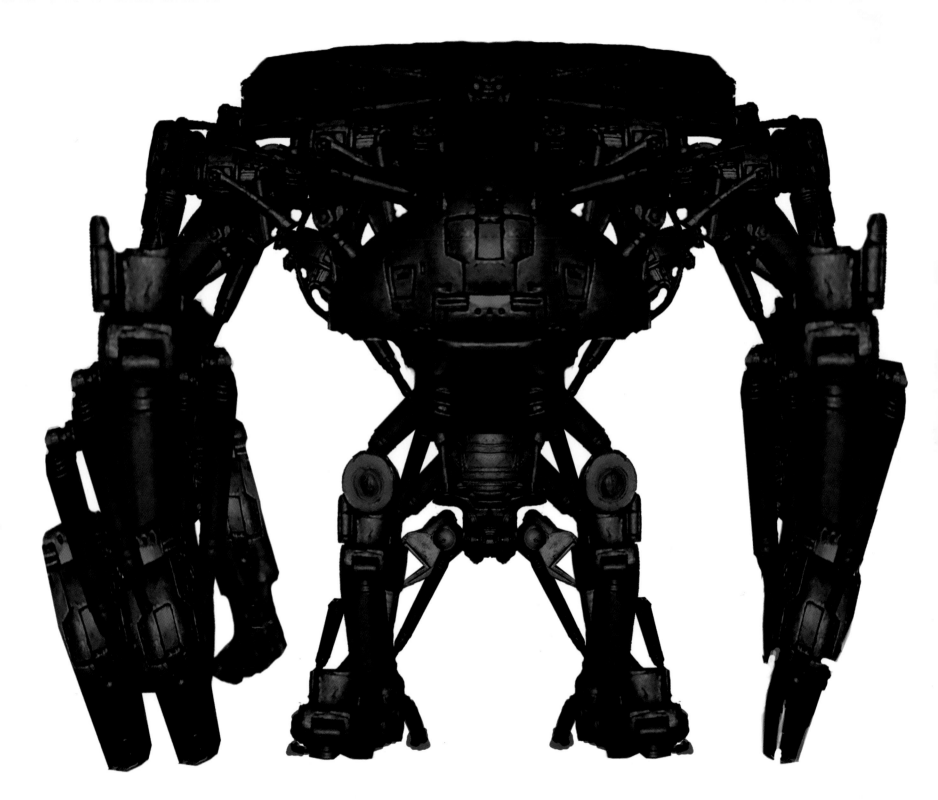

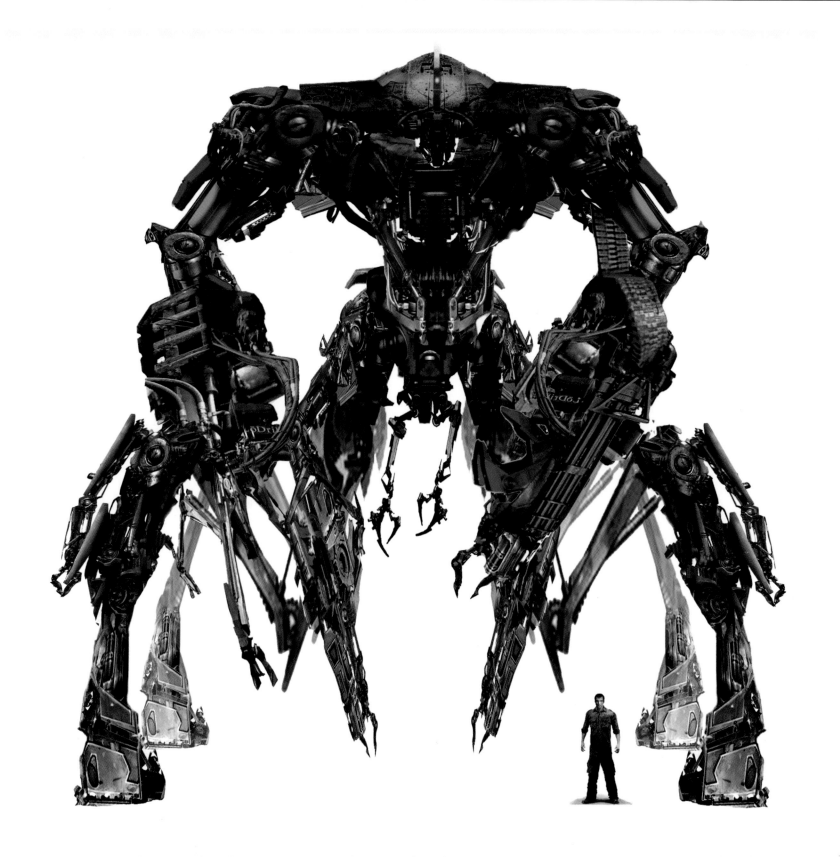

From tall to squat and tank-like to organic, Laing says they tried everything to hit the final look. "We wanted it to be a standalone design so that's why we tweaked it in so many directions, just to get some different styles to it."

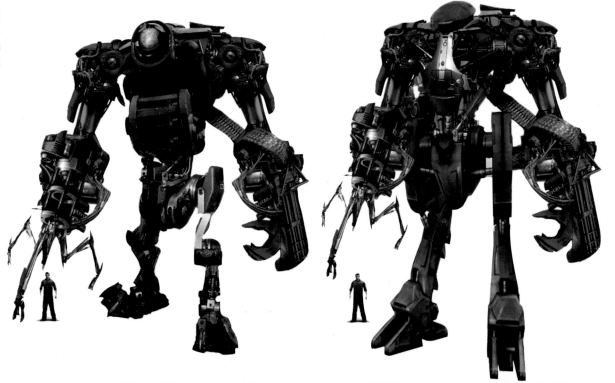

At one point the designs even went back to early scripts, Laing says. "The original script actually calls the Harvester out as being an insect, but then when you get into the way Terminators were built, I don't believe an insect would have been the way Skynet would have built them." Plus the insect designs elicited their own issues, specifically the spider design (seen on the opposite page) which turned out too similar to the mechanical spider used in the climax of the Will Smith movie, *Wild Wild West*…an allusion no one wanted to draw.

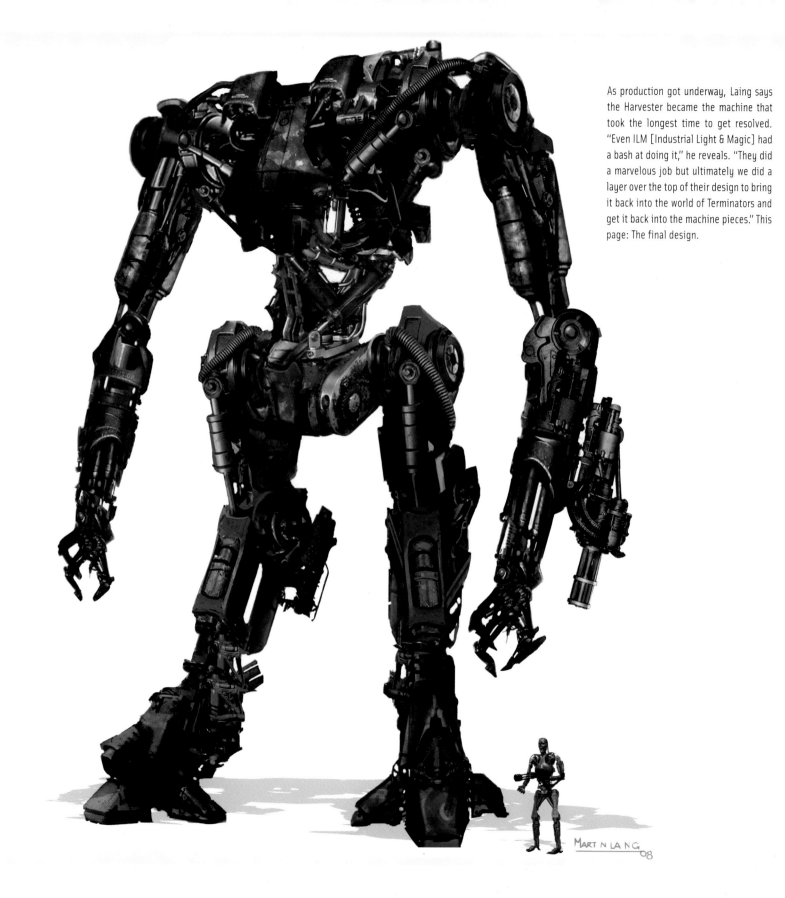

As production got underway, Laing says the Harvester became the machine that took the longest time to get resolved. "Even ILM [Industrial Light & Magic] had a bash at doing it," he reveals. "They did a marvelous job but ultimately we did a layer over the top of their design to bring it back into the world of Terminators and get it back into the machine pieces." This page: The final design.

MARTIN LAING '08

TOW TRUCK

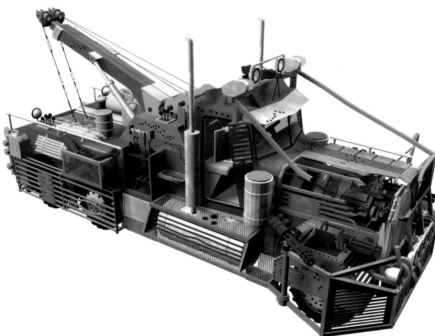

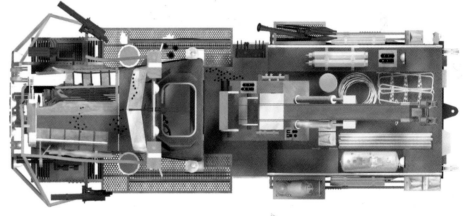

The heavily modified tow truck that Marcus uses to escape the Moto-Terminators was constructed to reflect the dire circumstances of the Resistance survivors. Laing explains, "As a member of the Resistance, obviously you are going to try and get whatever you can to keep yourself alive for as long as you can when having to do battle against Terminators. Here what we're saying is that these people have taken the biggest, baddest truck they could find and armored it to the teeth. If they need an extra gas tank, they have to weld it to the side. If they need guns, they also need to be welded. It has to be as big and beefy as possible to keep them alive." Built on the chassis of four actual Peterbilt trucks, Laing says, "We were then able to work off them, ripping them to pieces and adding that *Road Warrior* feel."

MOTO-TERMINATORS

As the tow truck races away, the Harvester deploys a new threat to give chase – Moto-Terminators. Small, agile and deadly, the Moto-Terminators detach from the Harvester to serve as ultra fast, riderless motorcycles for precision attacks. The following storyboard panels chart Marcus, Kyle and Star's thrilling escape as they navigate through the abandoned cars littering the now-desolate highway. Like the Harvester, the Moto-Terminators went through a long design process, shown over the following pages, before a final choice was made.

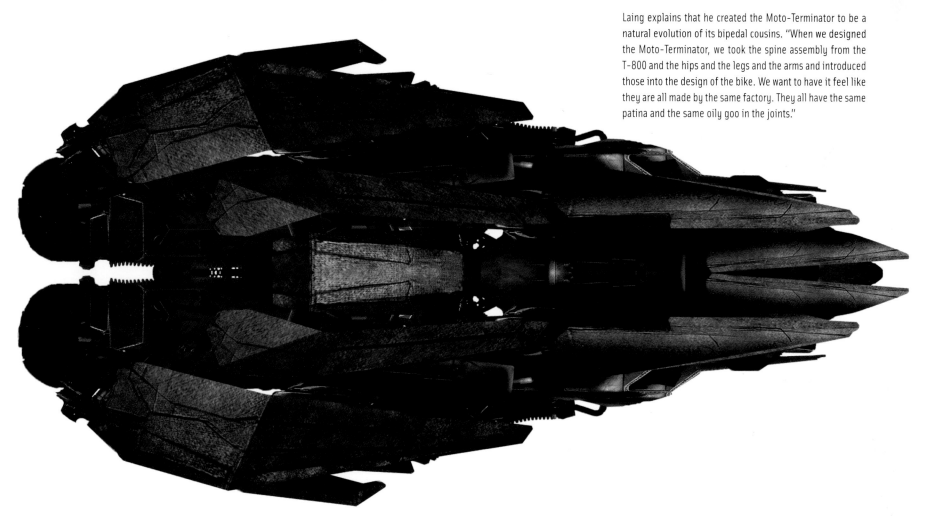

Laing explains that he created the Moto-Terminator to be a natural evolution of its bipedal cousins. "When we designed the Moto-Terminator, we took the spine assembly from the T-800 and the hips and the legs and the arms and introduced those into the design of the bike. We want to have it feel like they are all made by the same factory. They all have the same patina and the same oily goo in the joints."

These images show an early design pass for the Moto-Terminators. "When we were first coming up with the idea, McG said let's just have a Terminator with wheels, literally holding onto the front and back wheels. We went down the road of doing that, but it started looking comical. Plus we wanted to turn this into something that could happen, with a certain power to it, so sticking wheels on Terminators got ridiculous. As we progressed with the design, it became more brutal and realistic in what you would have to do to engineer a bike to work like this."

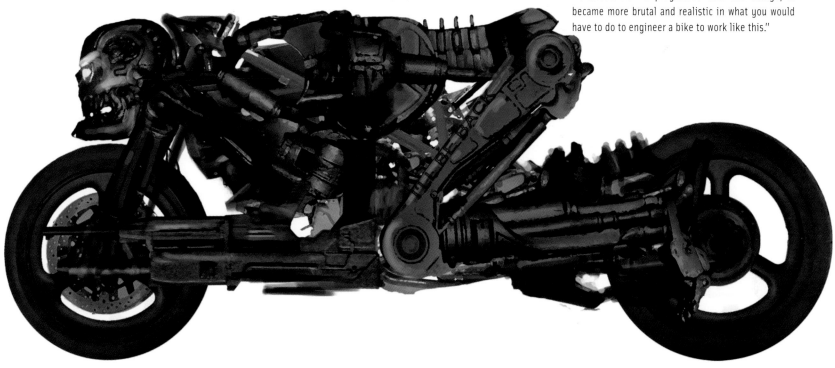

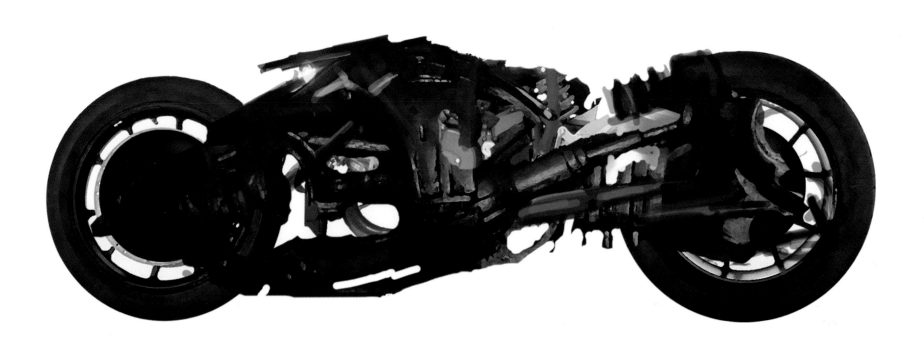

As the designs progressed, Laing was able to integrate more pieces from the Terminator endoskeletons into the Moto-Terminator frames.

Certain Moto-Terminator designs such as these were rejected for being too utilitarian and not menacing enough.

Next spread: The final design.

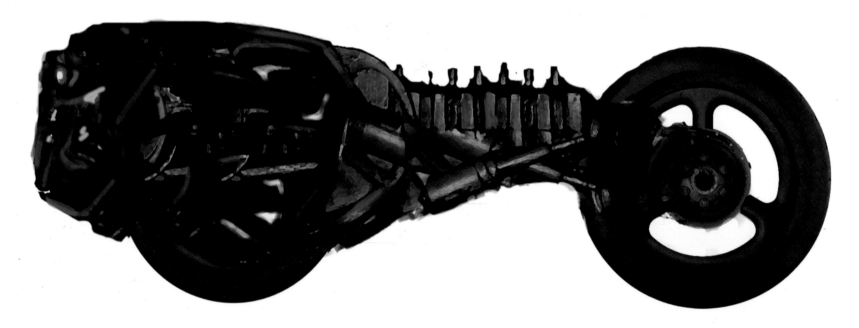

MINIGUNS ROTATE
TO ACT AS A
COUNTER-BALANCE
AS BIKE LEANS

FRONT MOUNTED GUNS
TRACK UP AS BIKE LEANS

TRANSPORT

After the Harvester plucks Kyle and Star from the truck crash, it deposits them into a Transport. These large passenger machines serve as the bleak holding tanks for humans rounded up by the Harvesters, in essence making them the futuristic equivalent of the Nazis' concentration-camp cattle cars of World War II.

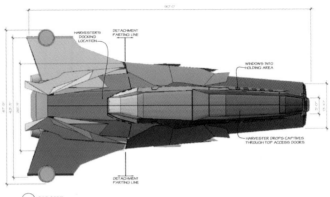

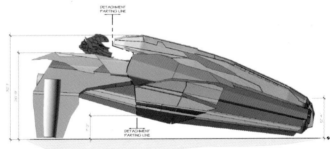

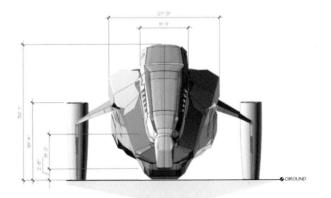

Speaking of his initial inspiration for the Transports, Laing explains, "There's nothing sadder than seeing a cattle car go by with all these sad eyes of the cattle staring back at you. So it was on a drive down the freeway of Albuquerque that I came up with the idea that people in the future are being used and abused like cattle, so let's use the same device. We have cattle cars that work today for this purpose so why wouldn't they be used in the same way in the future?"

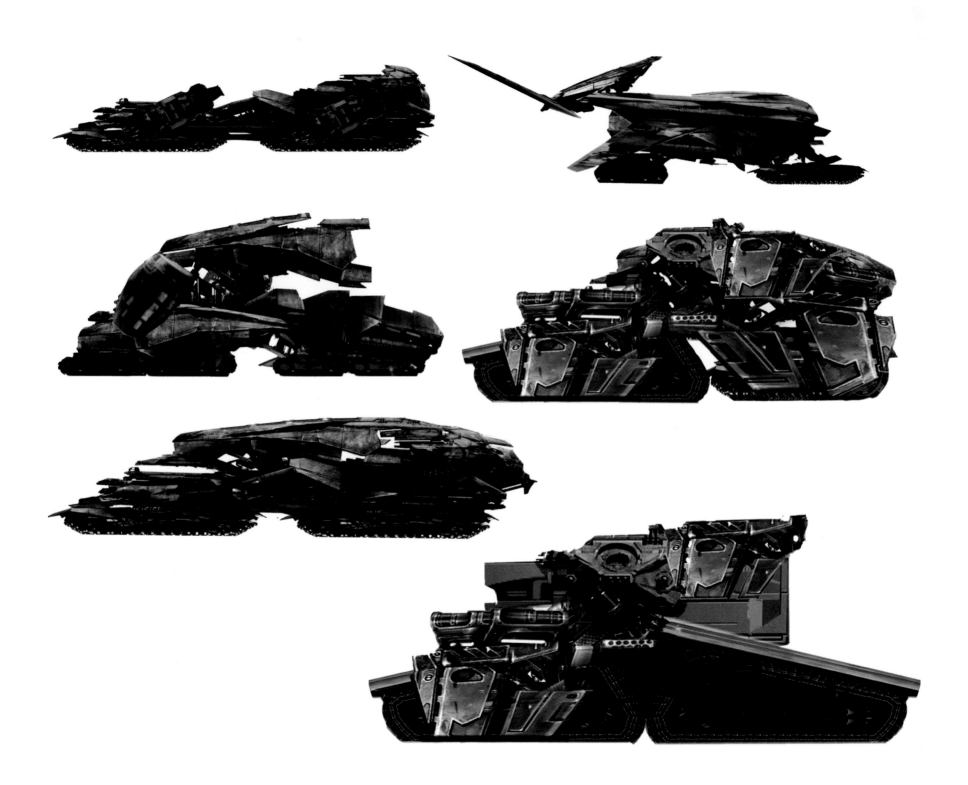

Laing continues, "With that in mind and knowing we had these forty-foot long boxes to work with, we then created a flying ship around these containers."

As seen in this painting, the size of the Transport provides the necessary space for the mano-a-mano battle between the Harvester and Marcus on the roof.

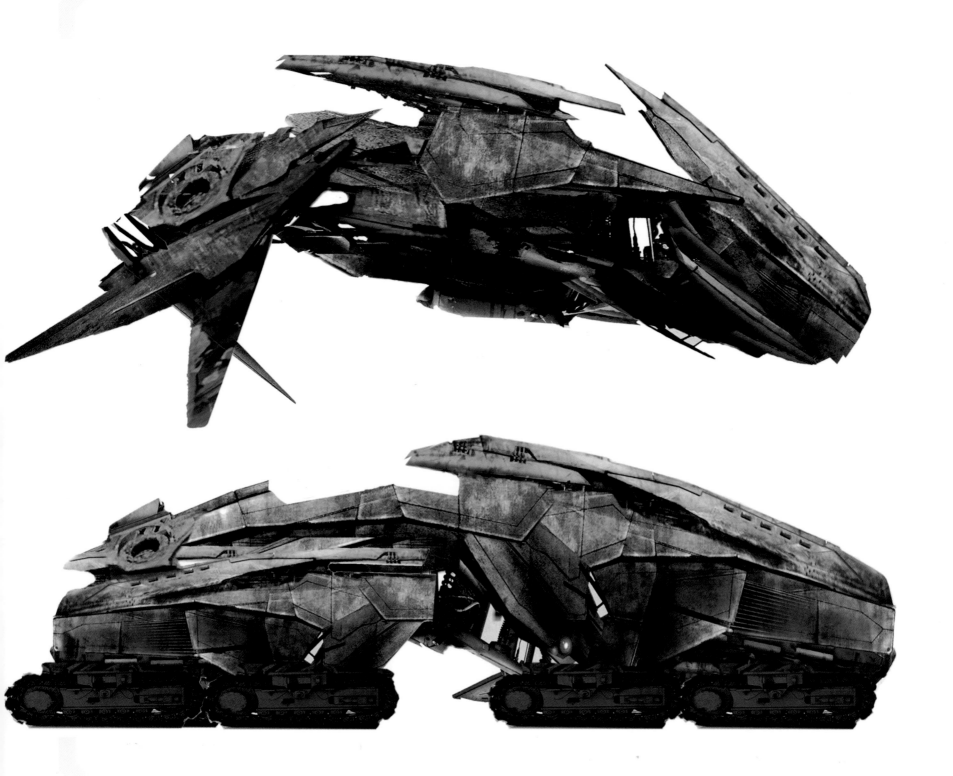

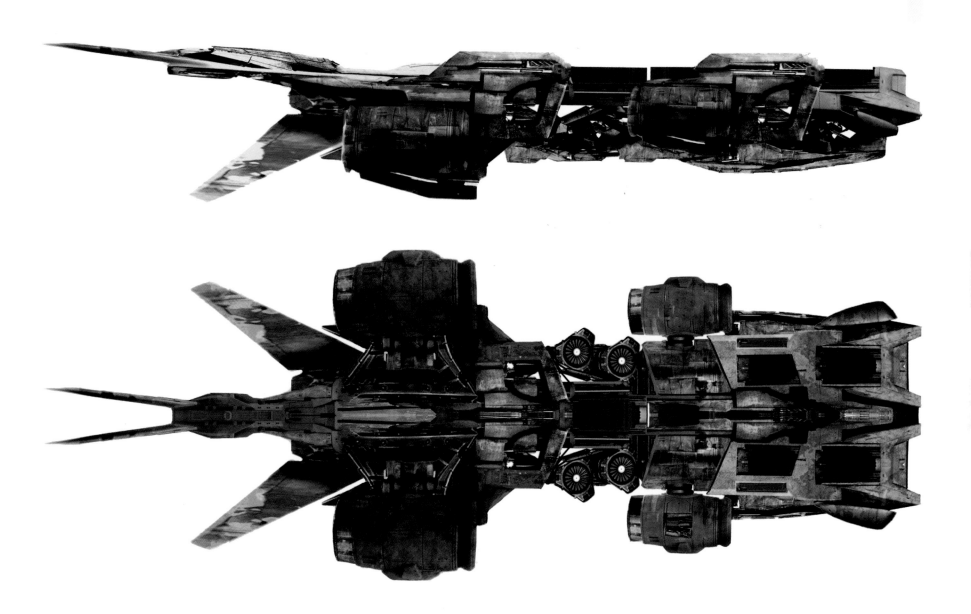

The final Transport designs also had to incorporate elements of the same machine as seen in previous films. "We wanted the vertical takeoff and landing that was used so successfully in the previous movies," Laing explains, "so we knew that we had to have a series of engines in the middle to keep it stable and a series of engines in the back to propel it. Using some physics and airplane design with the cattle car foundation, we put it all together like an Erector set."

Nose Art

In a brief sequence where the Resistance soldiers prepare for battle, there is a glimpse inside the airplane hangar with A-10 Warthogs personalized with WWII-era nose art. The "Boar U2 Death" art signifies Resistance pilot Blair Williams' plane. Laing says, "In a world where everything has fallen apart, they're making a silk purse out of a pig's ear. She is trying to do something to make it prettier and to make it hers."

In this concept painting, Marcus desperately fights to disengage the Harvester's deadly claw as it drags the both of them to their watery grave at the bottom of the river.

In this storyboard sketch and detailed concept painting, Marcus stares in horror as the engine of an A-10 is about to violently slam into the river and take him under.

MCKINNON

After surviving the river, Marcus comes upon the pilot of the downed A-10 dangling in the air from her parachute. Blair Williams is alive and Marcus climbs up to cut her free. Laing explains the original storyboards and concept painting changed dramatically during production. "In our journeys we went up to an area just above Santa Fe where there had been a lot of forest fires and natural devastation. We walked around in this very post-apocalyptic world of post-forest fire. We thought it was the perfect environment for her to land, maybe suspended on a tower." Ultimately though, the logistics of the shoot meant a location nearer to the film's Albuquerque base was necessary. "I drove around with McG and came up with this wonderful sandy environment. We took the same idea of the power tower but just transferred it to this new location."

FINDING BLAIR

These images chart the major set piece locations that form a backdrop as Blair and Marcus forge a bond during their travels back to the Resistance Outpost.

LOADING ZONE

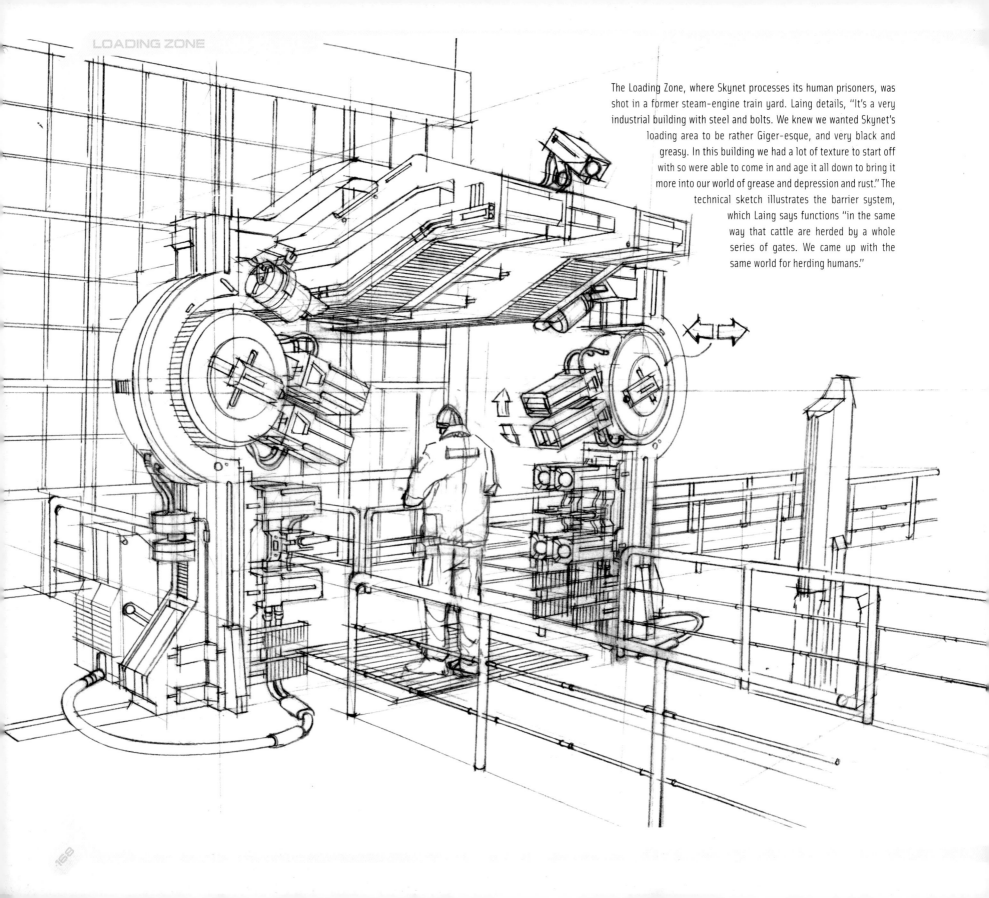

The Loading Zone, where Skynet processes its human prisoners, was shot in a former steam-engine train yard. Laing details, "It's a very industrial building with steel and bolts. We knew we wanted Skynet's loading area to be rather Giger-esque, and very black and greasy. In this building we had a lot of texture to start off with so were able to come in and age it all down to bring it more into our world of grease and depression and rust." The technical sketch illustrates the barrier system, which Laing says functions "in the same way that cattle are herded by a whole series of gates. We came up with the same world for herding humans."

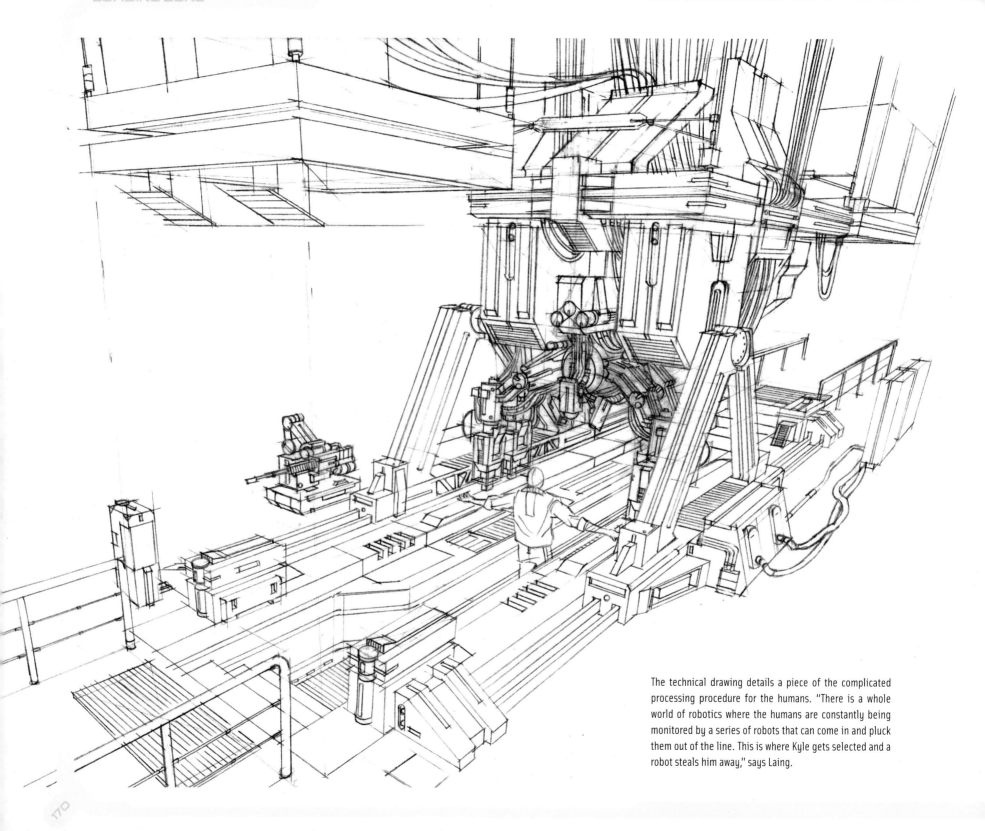

The technical drawing details a piece of the complicated processing procedure for the humans. "There is a whole world of robotics where the humans are constantly being monitored by a series of robots that can come in and pluck them out of the line. This is where Kyle gets selected and a robot steals him away," says Laing.

RESISTANCE
OUTPOST

The storyboards lay out the pivotal moment when Marcus steps onto the Resistance Outpost grounds and triggers a landmine meant to warn the soldiers of a Terminator sector breach. The behind-the-scenes photo shows the stunt as it happened on set.

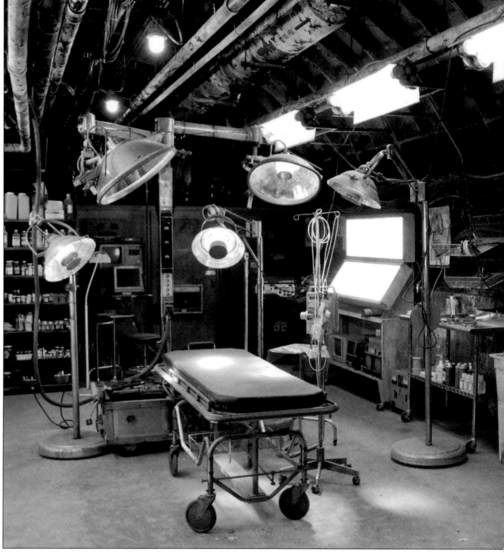

Marcus wakes inside the makeshift Outpost hospital. Set decorator Victor Zolfo explains great thought went into creating this important space. "We were thinking this installation [an old missile silo] had never had a hospital or an infirmary, so everything would have had to have been brought in. We imagined what it would be like to go to a bombed-out hospital and find some operating room lights and a bunch of medical and tech equipment and then drag it back. And they would have to weld it into something that would be able to function as a makeshift surgery. Actually, my favorite object in the whole movie is this crazy operating room light [pictured above] that my guys built for the Outpost surgery. It's made with car batteries and generators and these big operating room heads that they articulated and are able to go in any position. It's a sculptural work of art and it really said this is what the Resistance is all about."

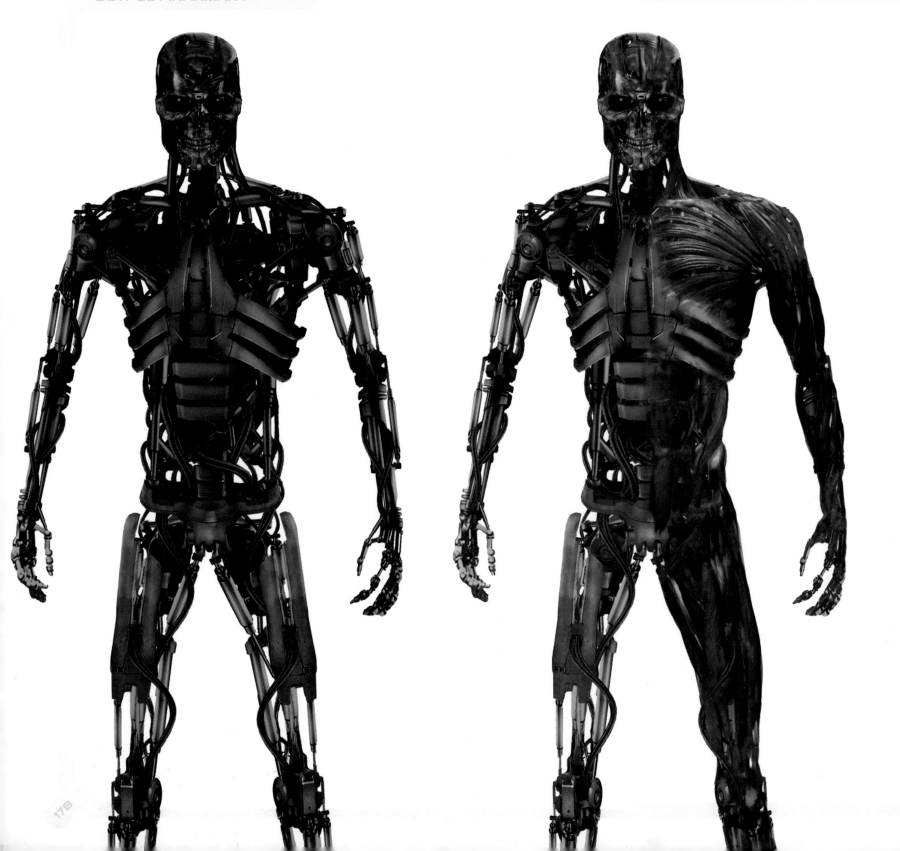

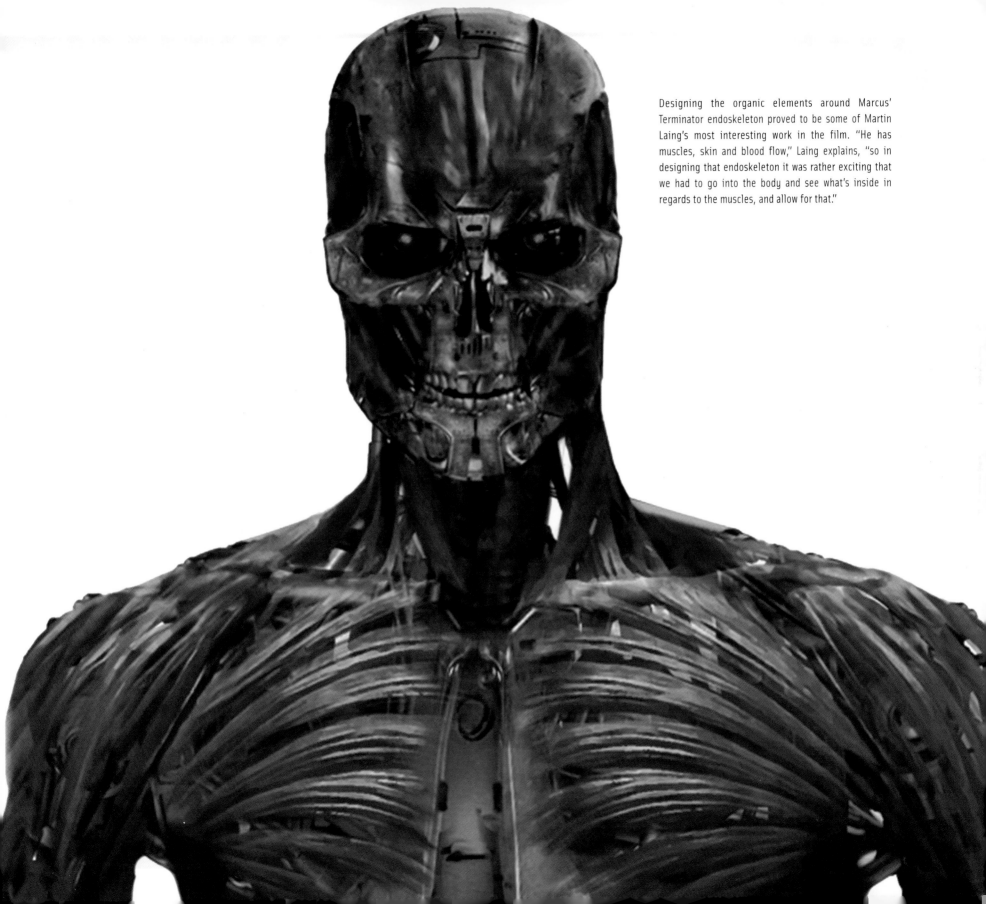

Designing the organic elements around Marcus' Terminator endoskeleton proved to be some of Martin Laing's most interesting work in the film. "He has muscles, skin and blood flow," Laing explains, "so in designing that endoskeleton it was rather exciting that we had to go into the body and see what's inside in regards to the muscles, and allow for that."

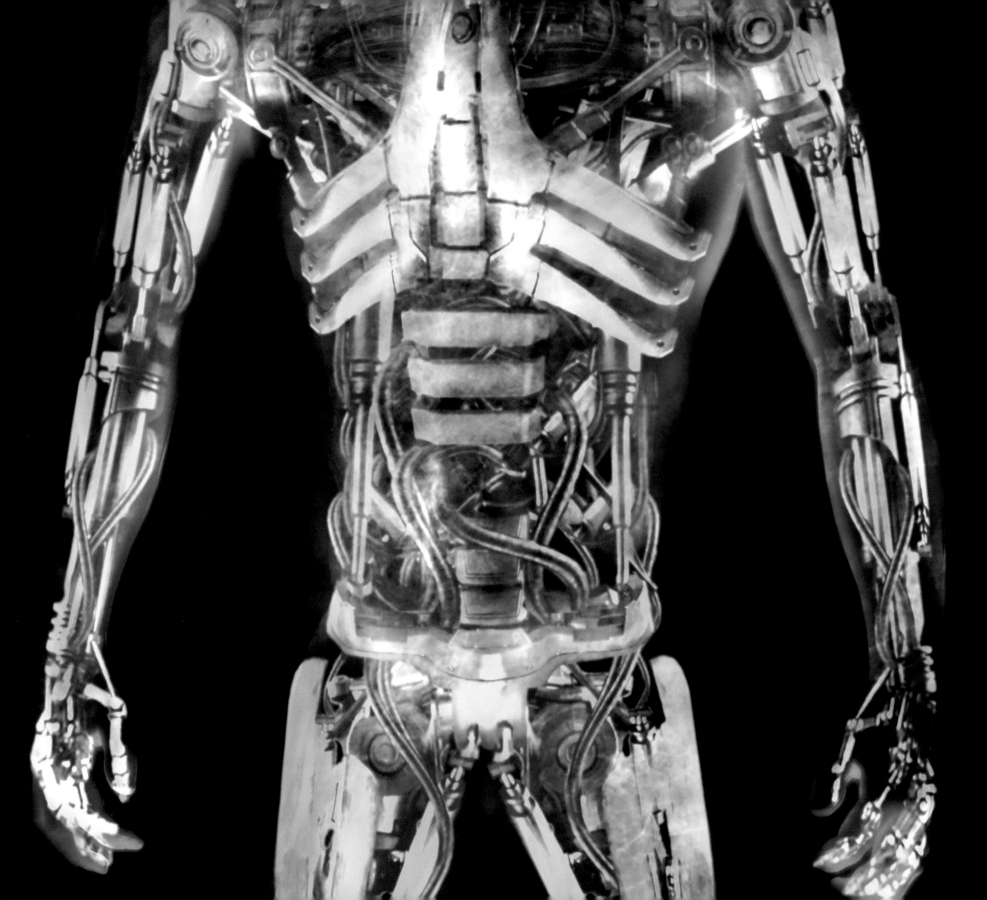

In keeping with the mandate for reality, Laing created all of his endoskeleton designs for Marcus with anatomically correct integrations. "We had to engineer our endoskeleton to work in conjunction with the muscles in the body so therefore the pistons that are there for the arm have to be a little bit smaller, because they have to allow for a bicep and triceps and a pectoral and all the rest."

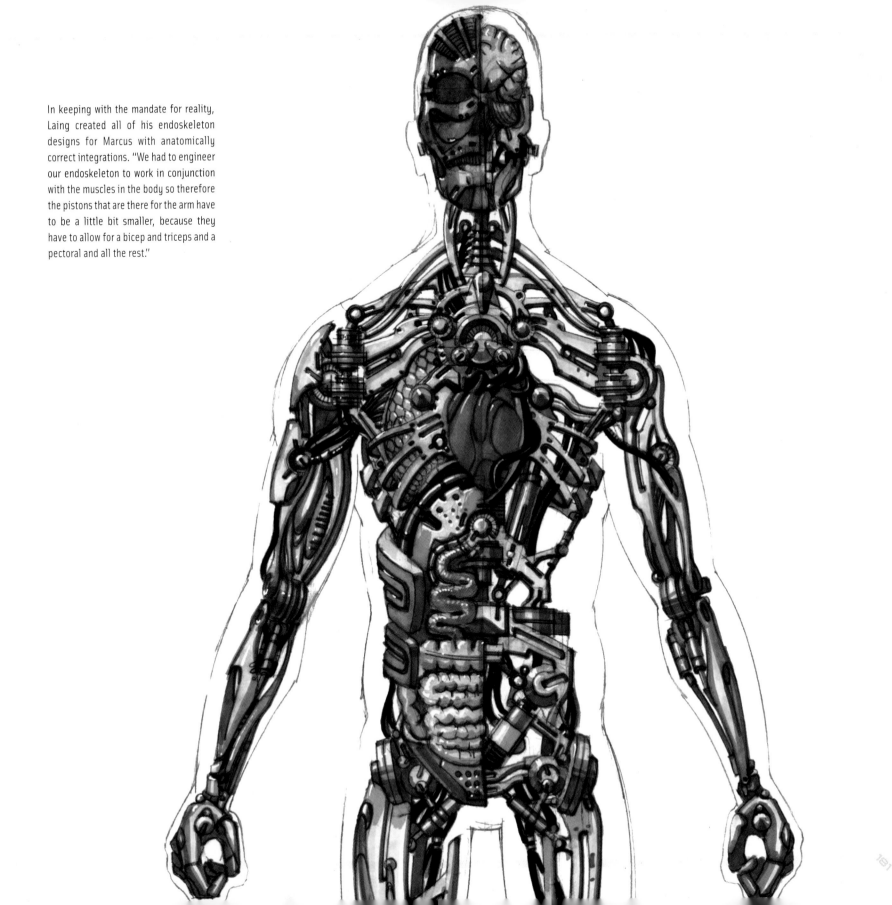

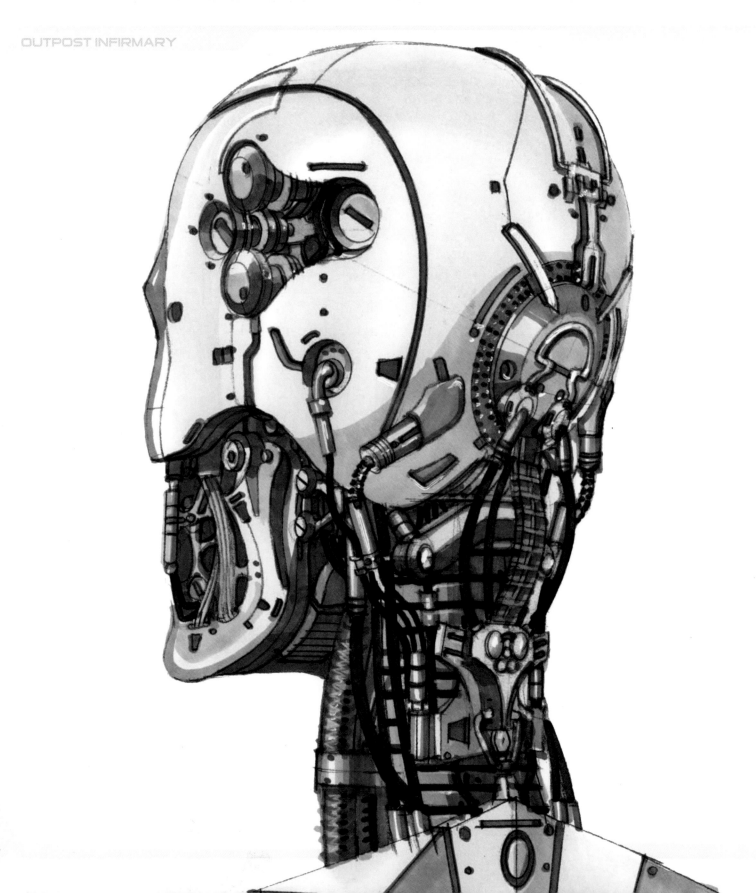

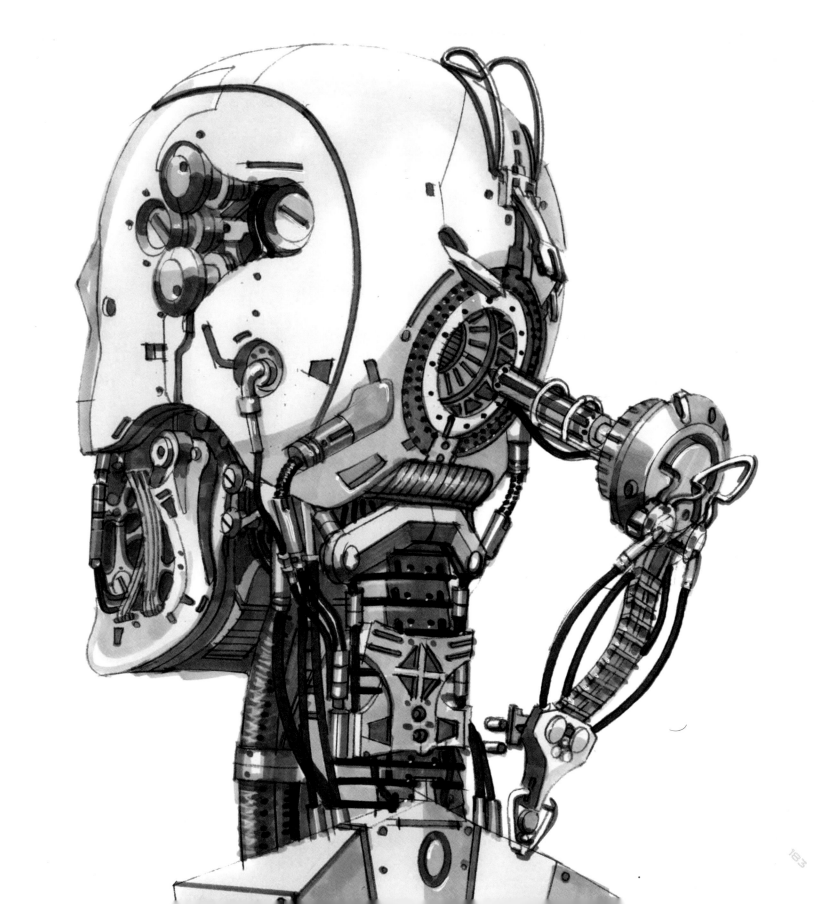

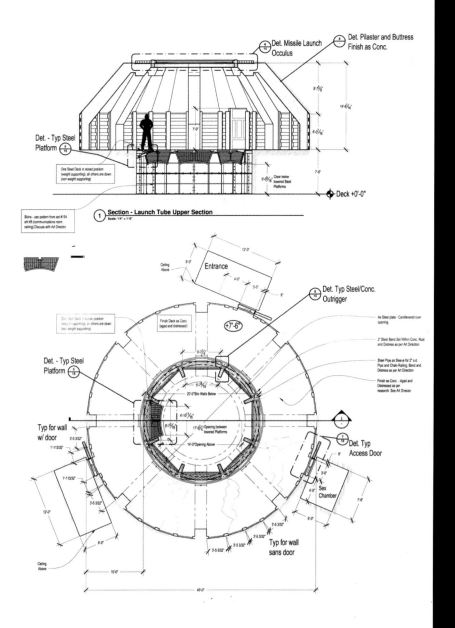

The dramatic pose of Marcus restrained and stretched out is one that conjures religious symbolism, but Laing refutes any subtext in the position. "You know we didn't even consider until we looked back at the paintings — that Marcus looks like he's being crucified all the time," Laing laughs. "We're not trying in any way to put any religious feeling into this. It actually all comes from a place of reality, like when Marcus is strung up [for interrogation]. I did a lot of research into how prisoners are strung up. The first thing you do with a prisoner is separate the hands, so we were designing around what they do today."

ESCAPE

This collage of concept art focuses on the dramatic lengths Marcus has to under-
take to escape John Connor and the Resistance so he can finish his journey north to
San Francisco...and Skynet.

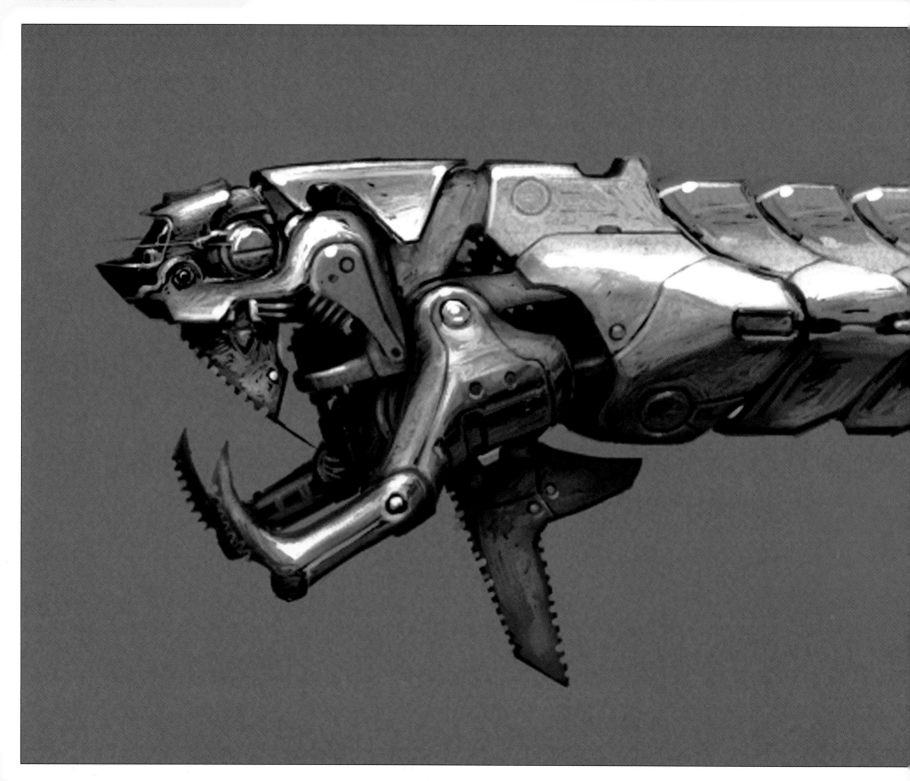

Perhaps the most convincingly designed incarnation of the Skynet machines, the Hydrobot is an inspired blend of organic form and mechanical function. Both John Connor and Marcus Wright battle the terrifying water bots in separate chilling sequences. "It's the first time we have seen a Terminator in the water," Laing explains. "And the Hydrobot has obviously been designed around the movement of an eel. We looked at eels and from that went back again into the reality of how you would make a robot like that work. It's not sci-fi silliness. We were actually trying to engineer these things." And based on Laing's intricate designs, Stan Winston Studio actually fabricated a functional Hydrobot for use in the production.

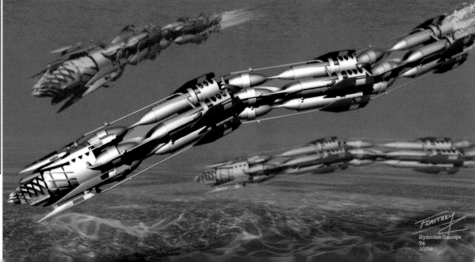

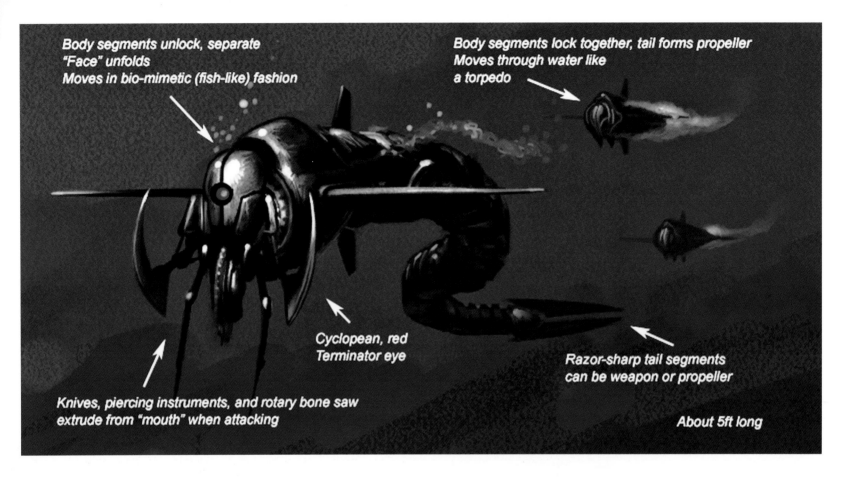

Body segments unlock, separate
"Face" unfolds
Moves in bio-mimetic (fish-like) fashion

Body segments lock together, tail forms propeller
Moves through water like
a torpedo

Cyclopean, red
Terminator eye

Razor-sharp tail segments
can be weapon or propeller

Knives, piercing instruments, and rotary bone saw
extrude from "mouth" when attacking

About 5ft long

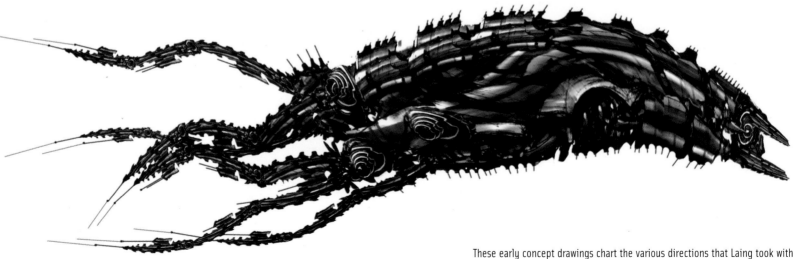

These early concept drawings chart the various directions that Laing took with the look of the Hydrobots.

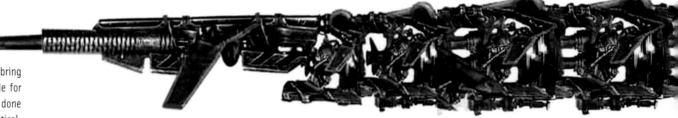

During the signal testing in the Outpost, the soldiers bring in a Hydrobot that will be slammed on a light table for inspection. Laing says the sequence could have been done with CG, but instead they where able to use a practical, full-length puppet version of the Hydrobot created by Stan Winston Studio. "It's those kinds of creations that make it a lot easier to act against," Laing adds.

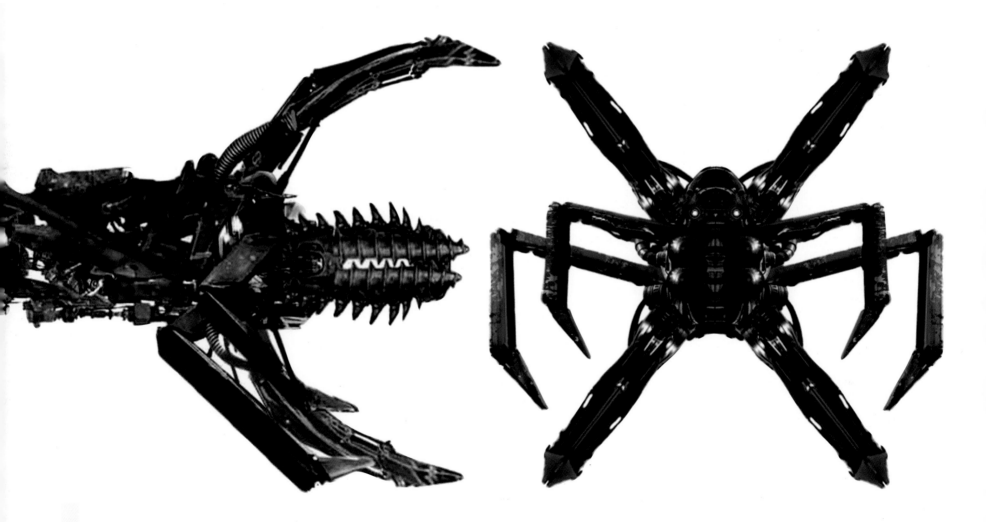

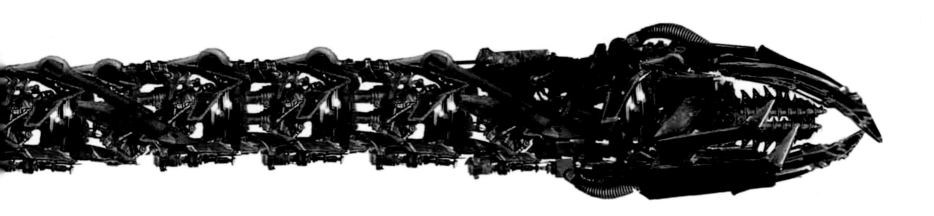

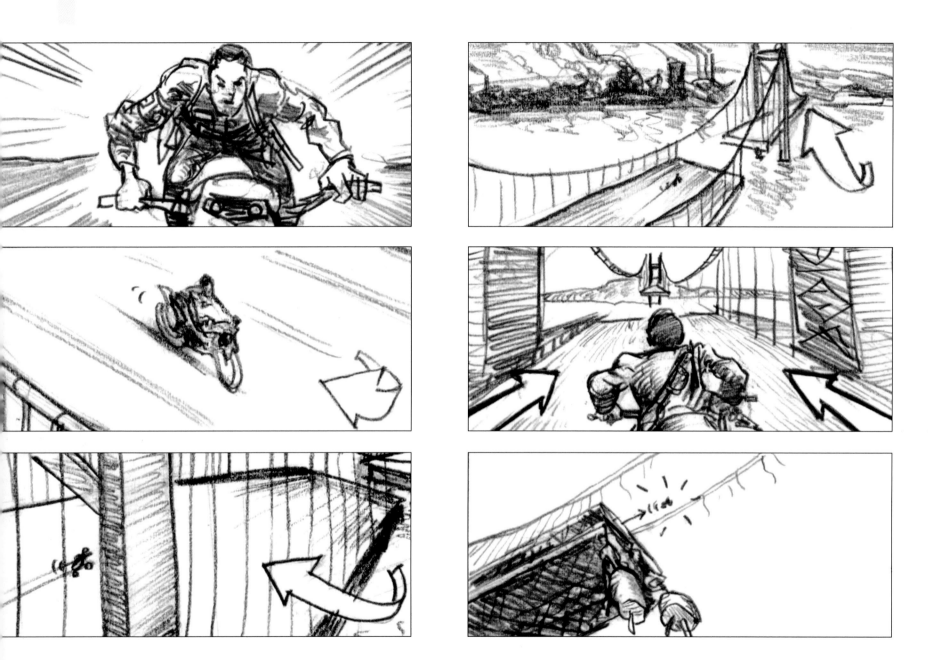

This set of storyboards details John Connor's harrowing Moto-Terminator ride to San Francisco — the heart of Skynet operations. Just as John reaches the first span of the Golden Gate Bridge, he realizes the road no longer connects to the other side.

The images depict Marcus' stealthy infiltration of Skynet Central as he manages to dodge patrolling T-600s.

Marcus wakens inside Skynet restrained by a robotic repair machine.
Following two spreads: Machinery used by Skynet to experiment on humans.

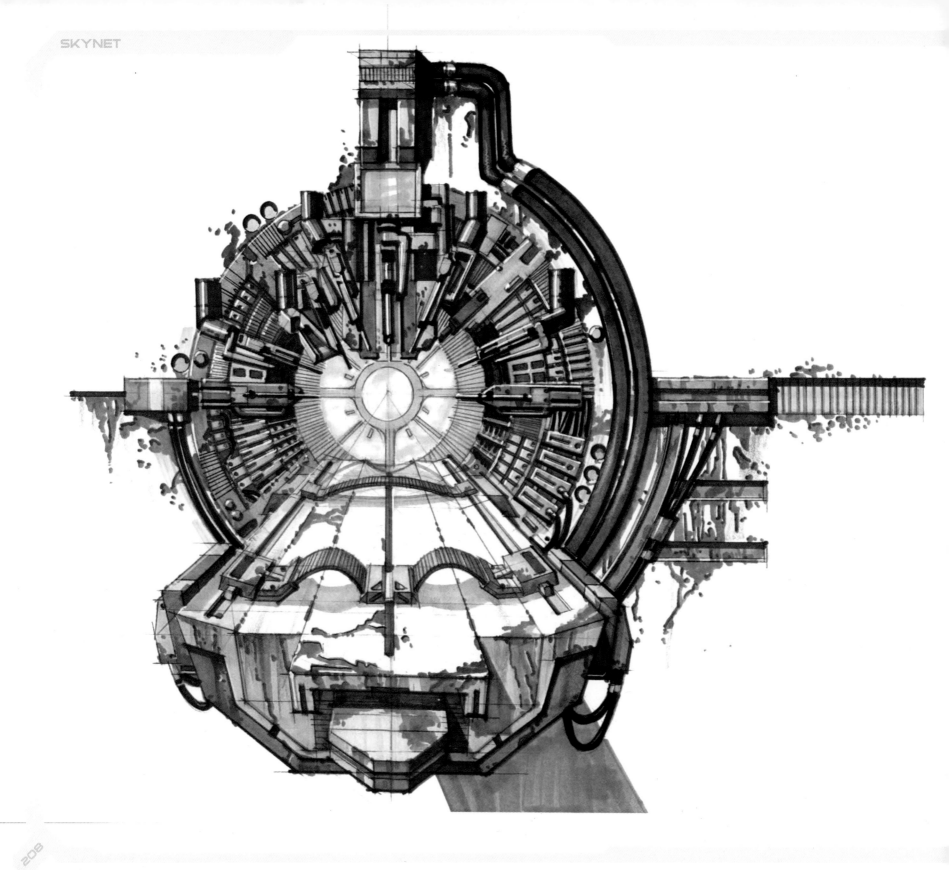

top view

bed

move apart

209

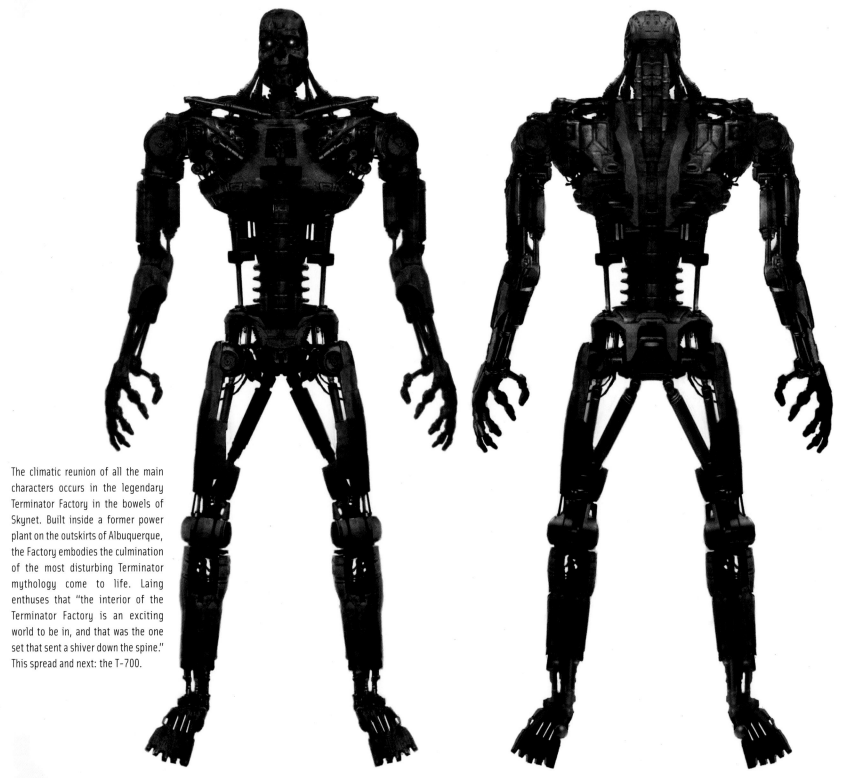

The climatic reunion of all the main characters occurs in the legendary Terminator Factory in the bowels of Skynet. Built inside a former power plant on the outskirts of Albuquerque, the Factory embodies the culmination of the most disturbing Terminator mythology come to life. Laing enthuses that "the interior of the Terminator Factory is an exciting world to be in, and that was the one set that sent a shiver down the spine." This spread and next: the T-700.

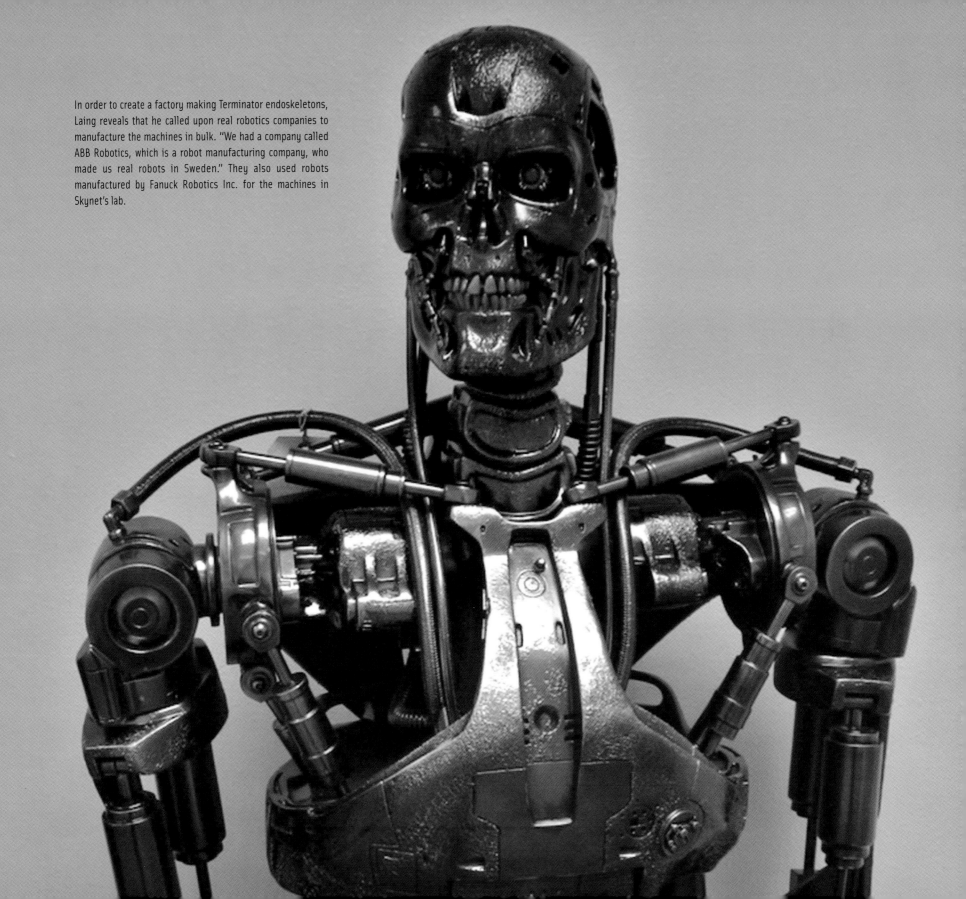

In order to create a factory making Terminator endoskeletons, Laing reveals that he called upon real robotics companies to manufacture the machines in bulk. "We had a company called ABB Robotics, which is a robot manufacturing company, who made us real robots in Sweden." They also used robots manufactured by Fanuck Robotics Inc. for the machines in Skynet's lab.

Concept drawings of the various machines that manufacture and forge the pieces for the endoskeletons.

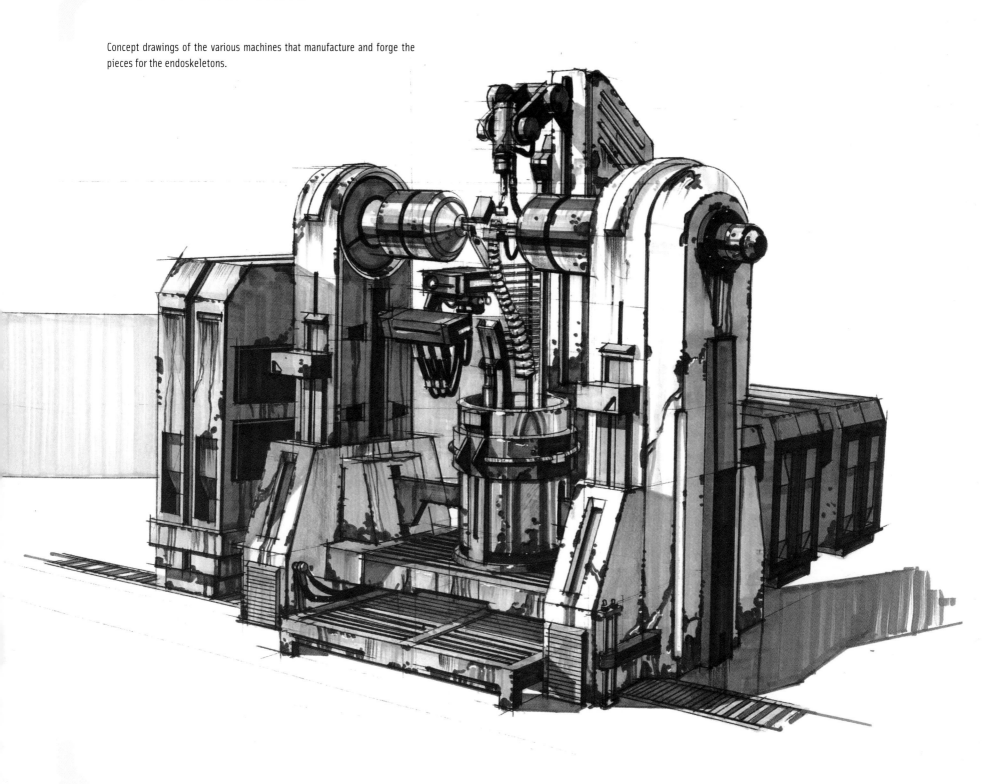

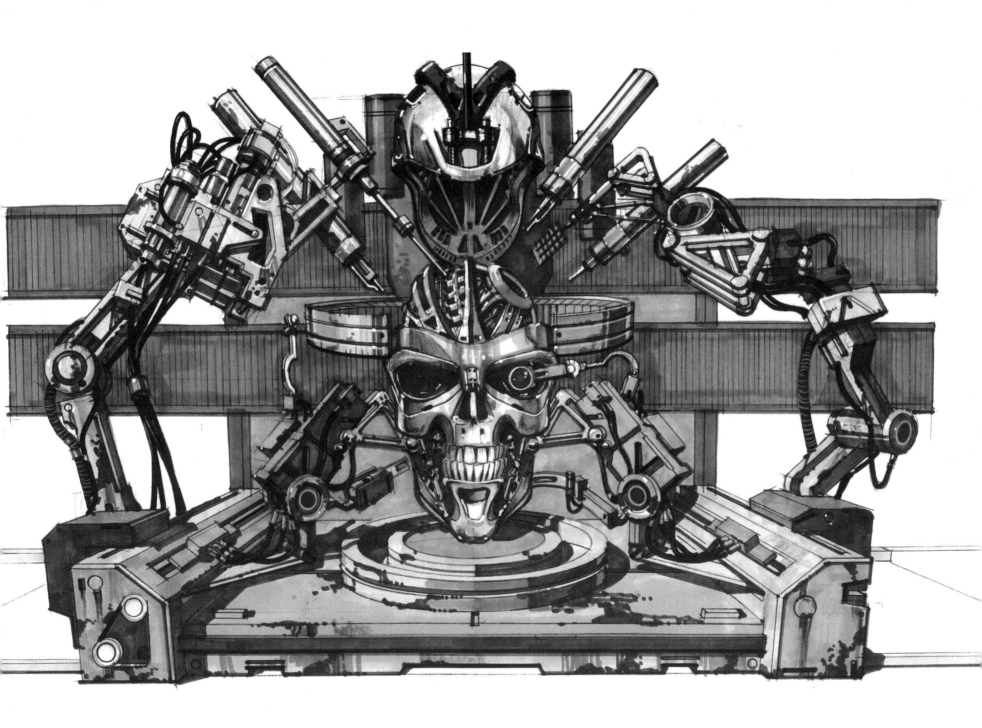

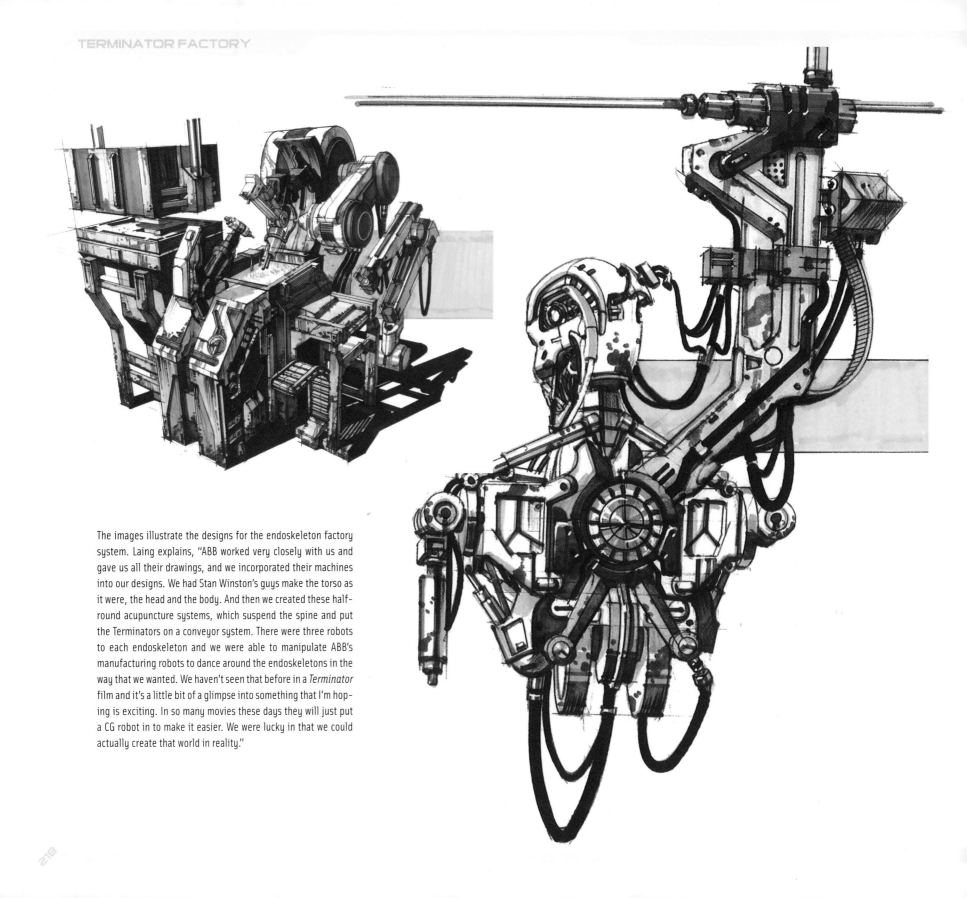

The images illustrate the designs for the endoskeleton factory system. Laing explains, "ABB worked very closely with us and gave us all their drawings, and we incorporated their machines into our designs. We had Stan Winston's guys make the torso as it were, the head and the body. And then we created these half-round acupuncture systems, which suspend the spine and put the Terminators on a conveyor system. There were three robots to each endoskeleton and we were able to manipulate ABB's manufacturing robots to dance around the endoskeletons in the way that we wanted. We haven't seen that before in a *Terminator* film and it's a little bit of a glimpse into something that I'm hoping is exciting. In so many movies these days they will just put a CG robot in to make it easier. We were lucky in that we could actually create that world in reality."

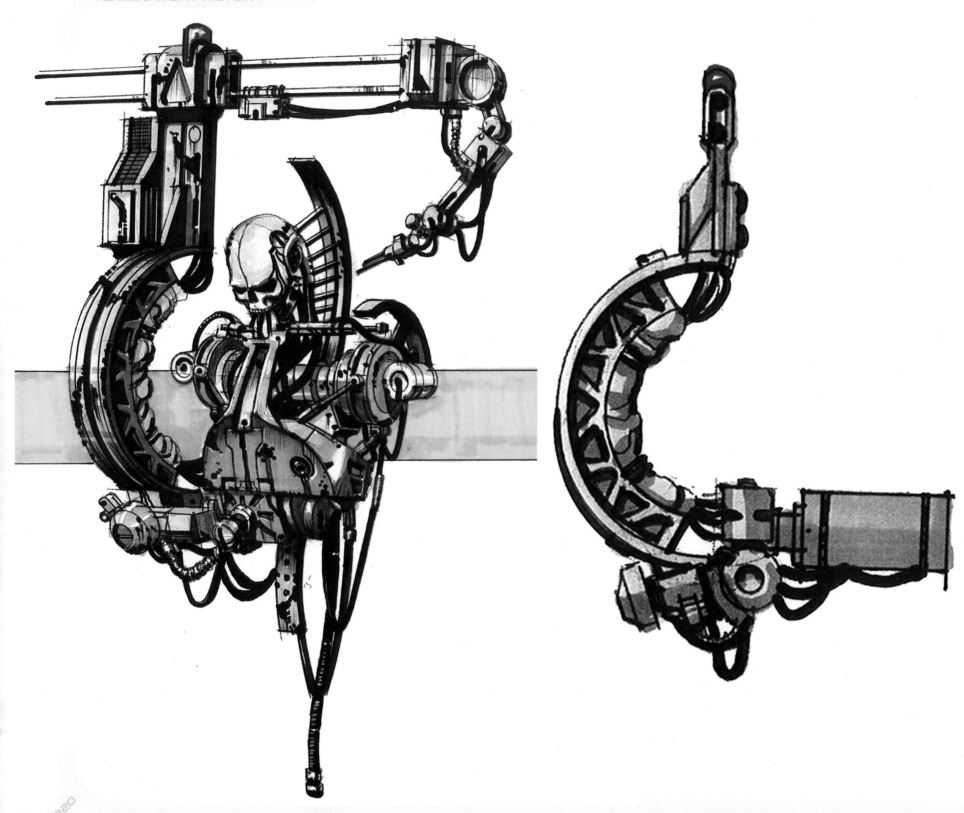

Deep inside the Terminator Factory, John Connor comes face-to-face with his worst nightmare. This key sequence, an epic battle between man and machine, sees the Terminator, which starts out in its fully 'fleshed out' form, become increasingly battle-scarred, until only the endoskeleton remains.

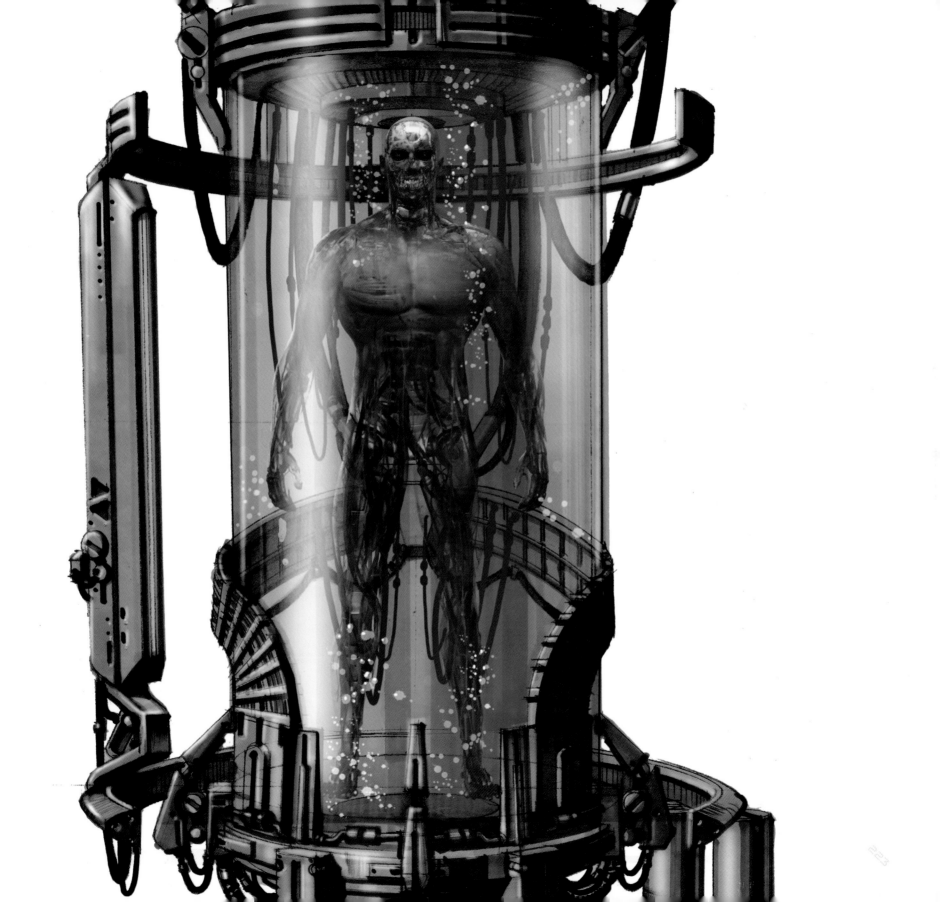

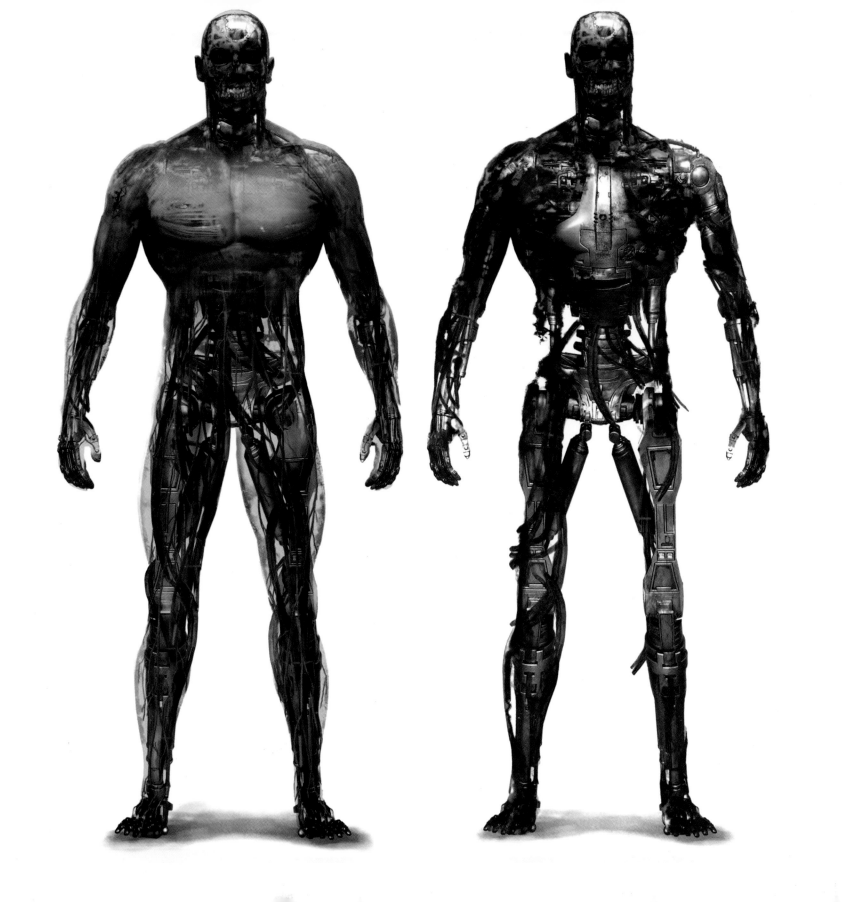

225

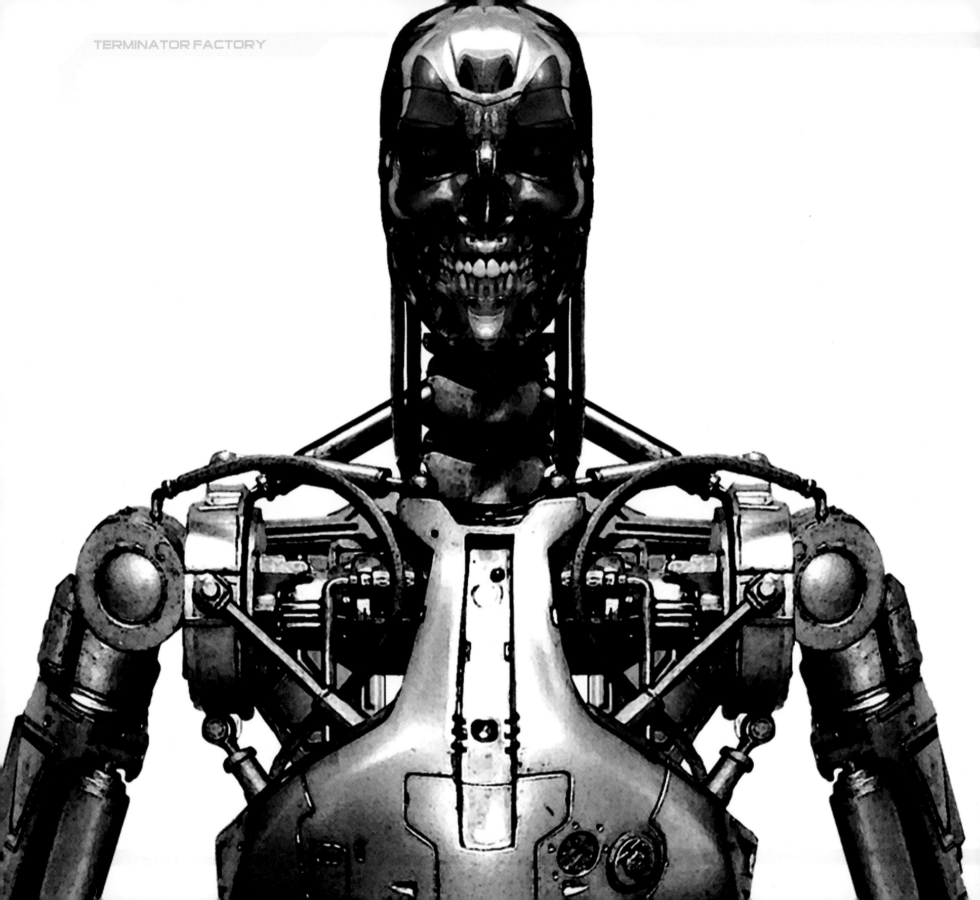

VIDEO GAME

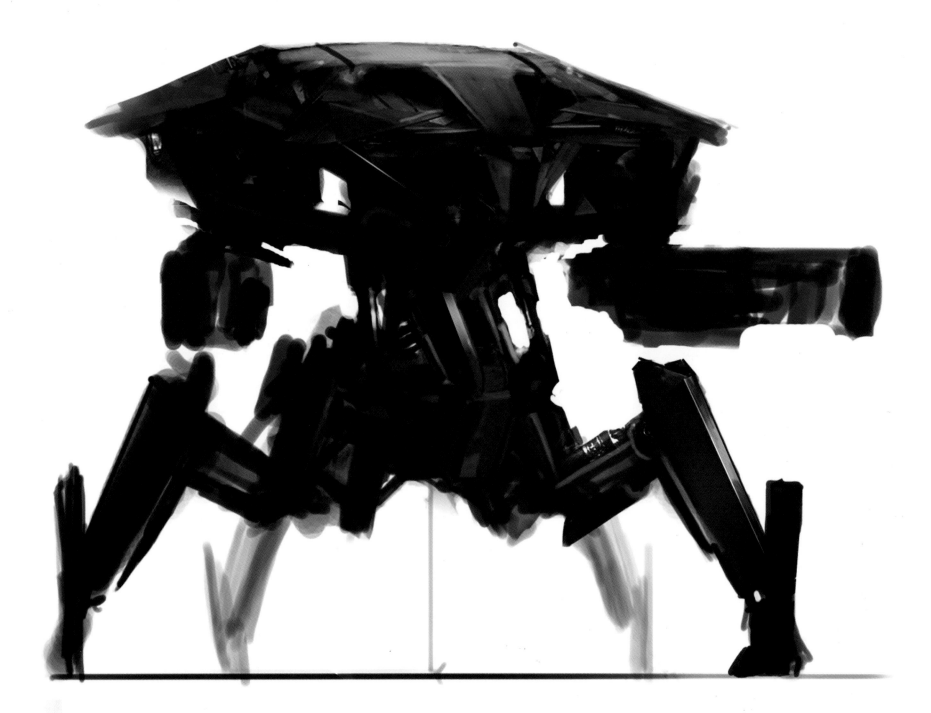

Rather than the industry standard of outside developers using production stills and style guides to produce a video game tie-in, the cross-platform *Terminator Salvation* video game is a unique project because of its close development ties with the film production. Cos Lazouras, the VP of production at Halcyon Games, explains that this game is created to be a proper prequel bridge to the film. "At the inception, I sent in two of the game's lead production designers and the art director. They sat with the film production team and literally worked side by side with them. Some of the stuff they created influenced the film, as well as the other way around." The concept painting on this page came from those early design meetings. "We also created some elements for the game that don't appear in the movie but are part of the universe," Lazouras adds. "We have the T model preceding the T-1 called the T-70 [see images above and left]. It's got four legs and the Resistance nickname it a 'Spider.' It's more of a scout — low level cannon fodder. It's very hard to kill though, and Skynet will send lots of them in."

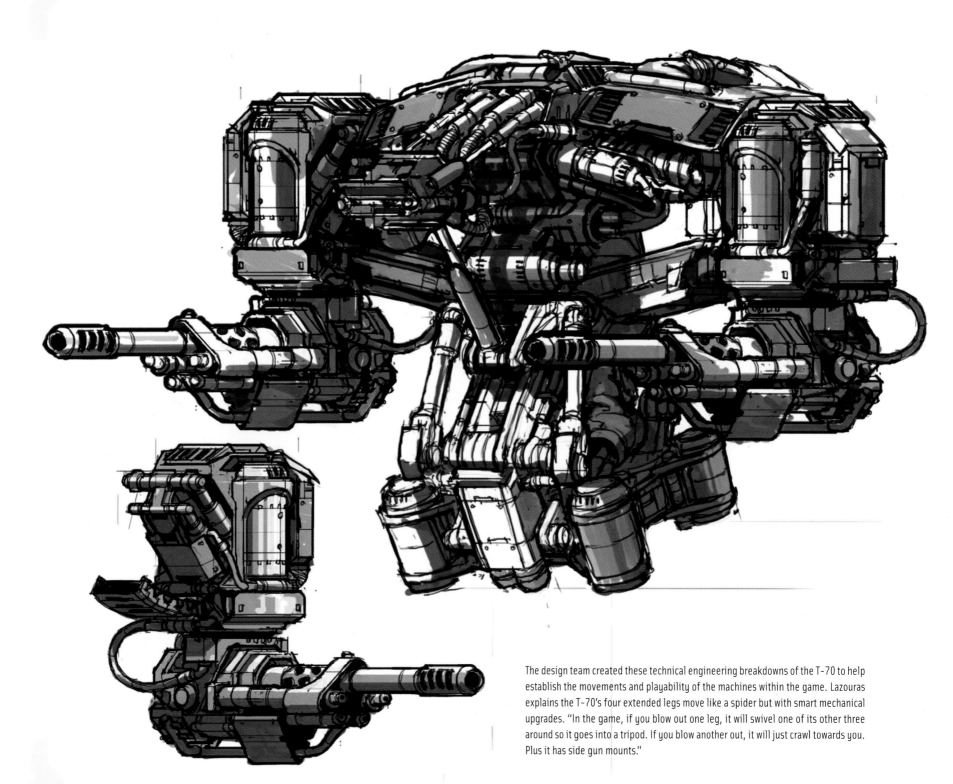

The design team created these technical engineering breakdowns of the T-70 to help establish the movements and playability of the machines within the game. Lazouras explains the T-70's four extended legs move like a spider but with smart mechanical upgrades. "In the game, if you blow out one leg, it will swivel one of its other three around so it goes into a tripod. If you blow another out, it will just crawl towards you. Plus it has side gun mounts."

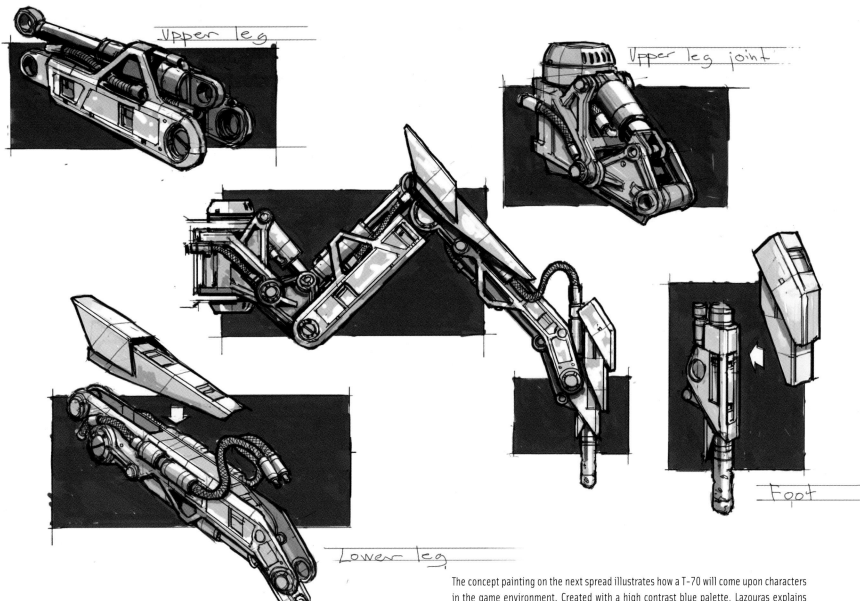

Upper leg

Upper leg joint

Lower leg

Foot

The concept painting on the next spread illustrates how a T-70 will come upon characters in the game environment. Created with a high contrast blue palette, Lazouras explains that "the art captures the original palette we were going for, but [the filmmakers] knocked back the blues in the movie because they wanted to get away from the look of the first two films. As we've progressed, it's changed back to a full color palette, but it's really desaturated. So the conceptual art has crept back into the game, especially with the mood lighting and the fogging. A lot of our conceptual art is how light plays in the atmosphere, so it's been retained. It's quite muted now because the game is trying to replicate the look of the film."

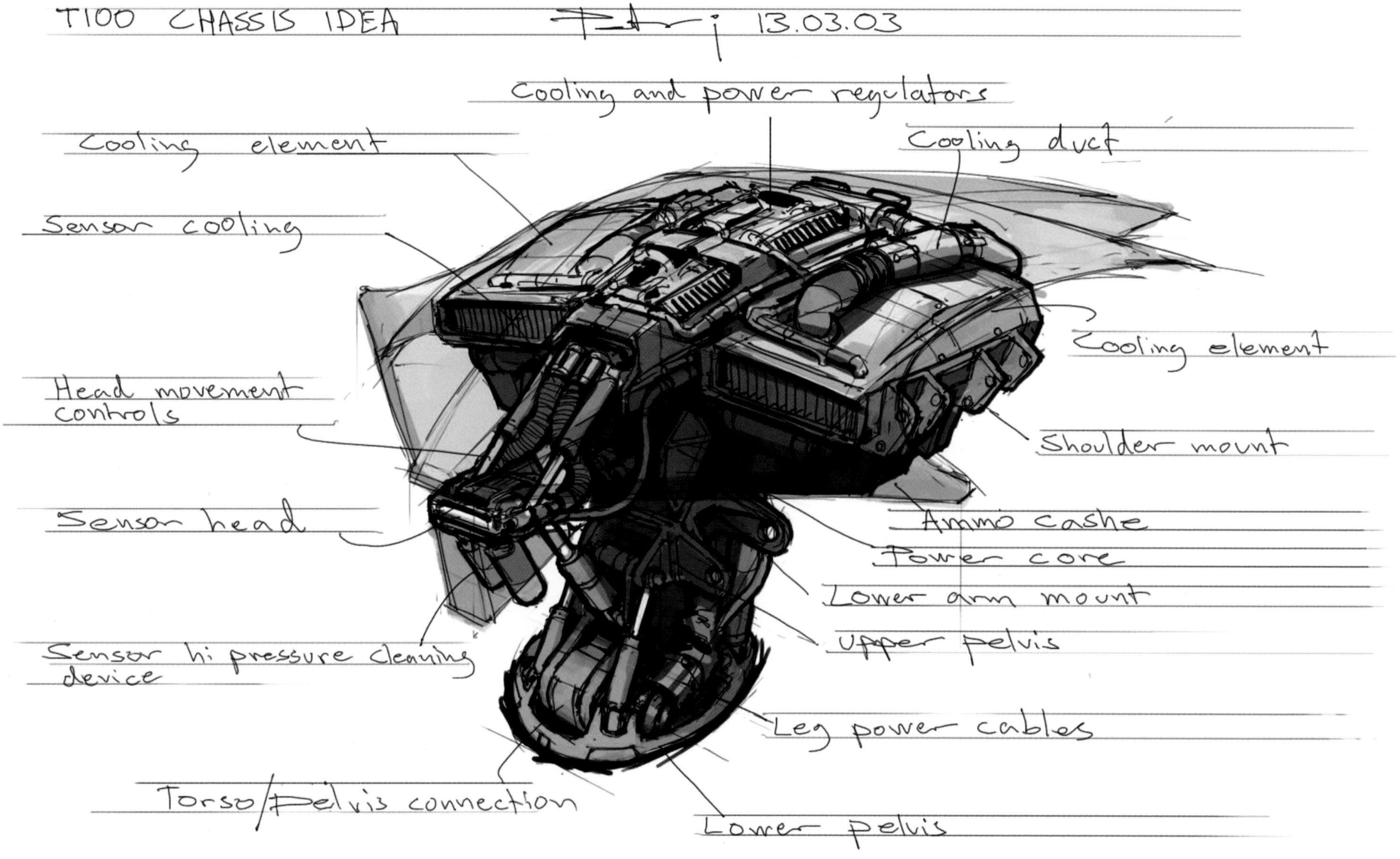

T100 CHASSIS IDEA   13.03.03

Cooling and power regulators

Cooling element

Cooling duct

Sensor cooling

Cooling element

Head movement controls

Shoulder mount

Sensor head

Ammo cashe

Power core

Lower arm mount

Upper pelvis

Sensor hi pressure cleaning device

Leg power cables

Torso/Pelvis connection

Lower pelvis

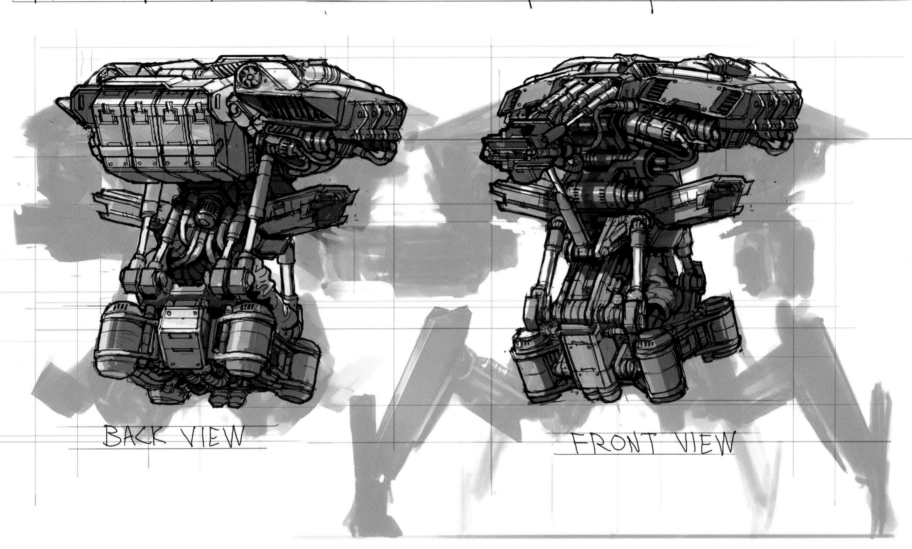

T100 TORSO   NO ARMOUR   28.03.08

BACK VIEW

FRONT VIEW

These are early design and engineering sheets for the internal
mechanics of the T-70 (originally called the T-100). The notes
reflect the core machine components and how they structurally
interconnect for mobility and function.

The game's storyline is set two years prior to the film. "It gives background on some of the events that happen in the film," Lazouras reveals, "and why various characters behave in the way that they do. It's a third person shooter like *Gears of War*. You play John Connor, and your team expands and contracts throughout depending on the scenario. The entire game is set in Los Angeles, and we've mapped it so you play from Eagle Rock to Downtown and West Hollywood. The city has been evacuated because of a really strong Skynet presence, and we show you why."

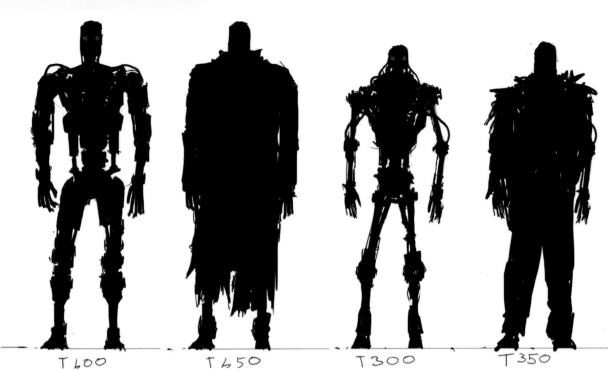

Lazouras explains this line up of Terminators was created early in both the game and the film's pre-production. "This was done when our artists sat with the team over on the film. They were doing silhouettes as to what the endos were going to look like and what model number they would be. They settled on the T-600, and the interesting thing is that the bigger it is, the older the model." Gamers will eventually face off against "skin-jobs and T-600s" in the game play.

T600   T650   T300   T350

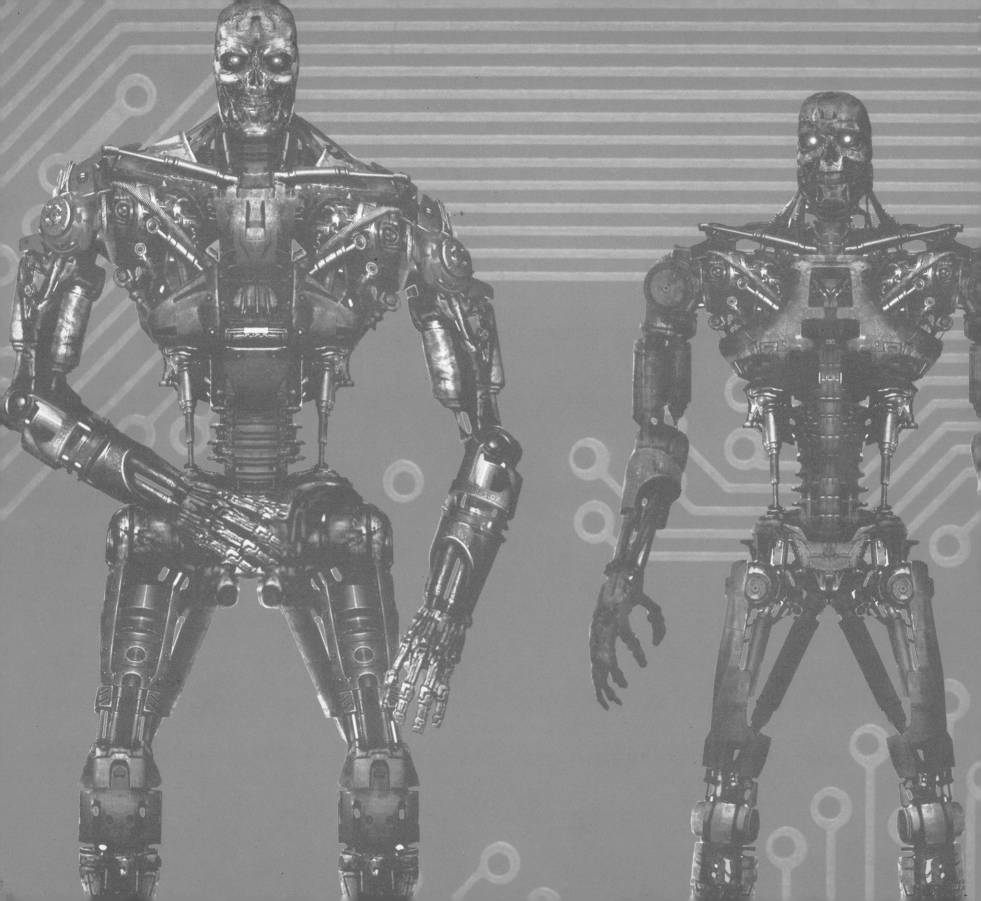